PORTRAITS OF

Kentucky Derby Winners

PORTRAITS OF

Kentucky Derby Winners

A 120-Year History

Paintings and Stories
by

Beverley Bryant

Health Communications, Inc.
Deerfield Beach, Florida

Originals and reproductions of the paintings in this book are available form the author.
For more information write:

Beverley Bryant
11312 83rd Court South
Boynton Beach, FL 33437

Publisher: Health Communications, Inc.
            3201 S.W. 15th Street
            Deerfield Beach, Florida 33442-8190

Cover design by Lawna P. Oldfield

*To Commander
Arthur Herbert Bryant, Jr., my father:
1912-1956*

B.B.

Acknowledgments

We wish to express our gratitude to the following persons for generously allowing us to reproduce artwork from their private collections.

Mr. and Mrs. Donald A. Fruehling—Jacket painting: Kentucky Derby, 1980
Mr. Stephen A. Grove—Aristides, 1875
Mr. James Ricciardi—Ben Ali, 1886
Mr. and Mrs. Jay Bashein—Riley, 1890
Mr. Robert Coleman—Ben Brush, 1896
Mr. Sanford Bryant—Pink Star, 1907
Sovereign Thoroughbreds—Old Rosebud, 1914
Sovereign Thoroughbreds—Regret, 1915
E.R. Bradley's Saloon—Behave Yourself, 1921
Mr. W. Cothran Campbell—Black Gold, 1924
Ms. Graciela Miti—Bubbling Over, 1926
Mr. Pepe Brown—Clyde van Dusen, 1929
Mr. James Ricciardi—Gallant Fox, 1930
E.R. Bradley's Saloon—Burgoo King, 1932
Mrs. Elizabeth Brooks—Brokers Tip, 1933
Mr. James Ricciardi—Lawrin, 1938
Mr. Peter Henderson—Hoop Jr., 1945

Mr. Michael Hirsch—Middleground, 1950
Sovereign Thoroughbreds—Dark Star, 1953
Miss Dana Goldsmith—Determine, 1954
Mr. and Mrs. Donald A. Fruehling—Iron Liege, 1957
Mr. Sol Garazi—Decidedly, 1962
Mr. Herbert I. Moelis—Forward Pass, 1968
Ms. Jeanne Burch—Canonero II, 1971
Mr. Harley Clemmons—Cannonade, 1974
Mr. Jacinto Vasquez—Foolish Pleasure, 1975
Gov. Hugh Carey—Seattle Slew, 1977
Miss Monique Yazigi—Affirmed, 1978
Mr. Sanford Bryant—Spectacular Bid, 1979
Mr. James L. Kerr—Genuine Risk, 1980
Mr. John P. Campo—Pleasant Colony, 1981
Hon. Paul Tonko—Gato Del Sol, 1982
Mr. John P. Font—Sunny's Halo, 1983

I gratefully acknowledge and appreciate the co-operation of Churchill Downs and thank Joe Hirch, lead writer for the *Daily Racing Form,* for his kind help and guidance.

Contents

Col. E.R. Bradley *whose Idle Hour Farm*
dominated the Kentucky Derby for 25 years

Foreword

In the spring of 1948, Calumet Farm was coming up to the Kentucky Derby with two exciting three-year-old colts: Citation, who won the Chesapeake Stakes at Havre de Grace, and Coaltown, who won the Blue Grass Stakes at Keeneland.

I had a great relationship with the late Ben Jones, who was head trainer for Calumet at that time. I'd ridden two Kentucky Derby winners for him (Lawrin in 1938 and Whirlaway in 1941) and we understood each other.

Actually, it was Ben's son, Jimmy, who was training Citation and the Eastern Division of the stable, while Ben had Coaltown and the Midwestern Division. I rode Citation to win the Chesapeake and was impressed with him. But Coaltown was also impressive in winning the Blue Grass under Newbold Leroy Pierson, and when I got to Kentucky shortly before the Derby all my hardboot friends were telling me that Coaltown was the better of the two and that I was on the wrong horse.

I'd done that number before. In 1942, while I was riding for Greentree Stable, I had my choice of Devil Diver and Shut Out for the Kentucky Derby. I chose Devil Diver and felt foolish when Shut Out won under Wayne Wright. Devil Diver eventually proved to be much the better horse of the two, but the consolation was long delayed.

I went to Ben Jones, probably the greatest trainer that ever lived. "Ben," I said, "I don't want to make a mistake. Tell me the truth. Am I on the right horse for the Derby?"

"Eddie," he said, "you've made no mistake."

That's a roundabout way for me to tell you that you've made no mistake in purchasing *Portraits of Kentucky Derby Winners*. Just like Citation, it's a winner. It's a tapestry of Kentucky Derby history from the first winner, the fabled Little Red Horse, Aristides, to Go for Gin, who won the 120th running on May 7, 1994.

They are all in *Portraits of Kentucky Derby Winners*; the mighty Hindoo (1881), one of the greatest horses of the nineteenth century; Regret (1915), the lovely filly who beat the colts and made the Derby a national institution; Black Gold (1924), perhaps the most colorful winner of all; War Admiral (1937), son of the Man o' War; Whirlaway (1941), who turned in the greatest finish in Derby history to win by eight lengths; Northern Dancer (1964) who brought pride to Canadian racing and breeding with his record-breaking victory; and those modern cracks Secretariat (1973), Seattle Slew (1977), Affirmed (1978), Spectacular Bid (1979), Swale (1984) and Sunday Silence (1989).

There is no race in the United States to compare with the Kentucky Derby for excitement and drama and Beverley Bryant, a talented artist and writer, has captured the scene with an innovative painting technique and colorful prose that enhances the glory of the times. I enjoyed it immensely and I'll bet you will, too. *Portraits of Kentucky Derby Winners* is 4 to 5 with me.

Eddie Arcaro
Miami, Florida

Note from the Artist

For portraits of horses from 1875 to approximately 1900 I had to rely on photographs of paintings done before photography existed or early photographs that were crudely touched-up. The paintings were in the elongated English style—the horses looked more like greyhounds—so I took the markings, head, expression and general conformation, and compressed the animal into a proportionate horse but maintained the old riding style and silks of the jockeys and the tack of the period. The backgrounds are completely authentic as well.

The book is made up of three sections. The first 35 illustrations are done in antique tones— sepia, antique green and old gold. In the 1920s and 1930s I introduce color, gradually increasing it until, by the 1950s, the images are full-color. The first 99 pieces are done with oil wash (turpentine and oil paint used like watercolor), which is applied before the detail is put in with charcoal. The paint goes on before the charcoal drawing.

The last section starts with 1973 and Secretariat and includes three Triple Crown champions, plus the filly Genuine Risk, and several horses that came close to the "Triple." Many of these are full-color oils on canvas.

PORTRAITS OF
Kentucky Derby Winners

Owner H.P. McGrath rests on the rail as Aristides and jockey Oliver Lewis go to the post. The original grandstand is in the background, with the clubhouse at the far left.

The first Kentucky Derby drew 42 nominations and 15 entries. The stakes were $50 from each entry with $1,000 added by the Louisville Racing Association, as it was then called. The trophy was a magnificent 300-ounce silver punch bowl valued at $1,000.

Ten thousand racing fans streamed out to Churchill Downs on this warm spring day. Many headed for the infield in horse-drawn wagons, buggies, carts and carriages. The clubhouse was a different scene. Ladies were dressed fashionably in long organdy gowns, ten-button gloves and large, elaborate hats. Bettors favored the traditional auction pools over the newly introduced pari-mutuel system from France, and bookies took bets as low as a nickel. Under the stands elderly black women served fried fish and chicken, while on the track 14 of the 15 jockeys going to the post were black.

The flag fell, the drum rolled, and they were off! Volcano took the lead, then eased back. McGrath's second horse, Chesapeake, broke last. At the half-mile pole McCreery led but soon fell behind Aristides and Ten Broeck. Aristides held the lead at the mile and McGrath, seeing his Chesapeake out of the money, signaled jockey Oliver Lewis to take Aristides in for the win. Aristides won with Volcano second and late charger Verdigris third. The time of 2:37¾ set an American record for three-year-olds, with 100 pounds up, over one-and-a-half miles. The "Little Red Hoss," as McGrath referred to his 15-hands-high colt, had won $2,850 for him, a rich purse for the day.

Price McGrath was a noted horse breeder and had earned for himself a colorful reputation. He had heeded the call to "go west young man," then settled in New York where he operated a gambling house. Returning to Kentucky, he established McGrathiana Stud. His white mansion became famous for burgoo feasts (a local stew) and he frequently opened his doors to the public.

Vagrant • May 15, 1876

Vagrant, William Astor's brown gelding with Bobby Swim astride, takes the lead from Parole. Two fashionably dressed ladies and a gentleman cheer their horse on.

The 6,000 people who made their way to Churchill Downs on May 15 anticipated a good time. It was a dry, sunny, perfect day. The men were most elegant in high glossy boots, white vests with cravats and derbies. They escorted ladies in long gowns that swept the floor.

The Derby had attracted the attention of many Easterners. Congressman John T. Morrisey of New York reportedly had wagered $1,000 but would not reveal on which horse. It could have been Parole, owned by tobacco magnate Pierre Lorillard, who was the favorite. Another New Yorker, William Astor, had other ideas. He had arranged just two weeks prior to the Derby to buy Vagrant from his Lexington owner, T.J. Nichols. In the event Vagrant won, Nichols would get the purse in lieu of the purchase price, at $2,950, a far better deal for him.

Colonel H.B. Johnson, the Tennessee horseman who had started the field for the inaugural Derby, was there to repeat his performance. The drum rolled and Parole shot out to the lead. At the half-mile, Vagrant was second but by the three-eighths pole had nudged into the lead. Parole faded badly at the finish and it was Vagrant by two lengths over Creedmore with Harry Hill third.

Vagrant raced until the age of ten, netting his owner some $13,875, a vast amount for the times, yet the honest gelding and winner of the second running of the Kentucky Derby ended his life pulling a cart in the streets of Lexington.

Trainer Ed "Brown Dick" Brown faces us as Baden-Baden with young jockey Billy Walker gallops past.

Newspapers from the major cities of the East and Midwest covered the third running of the Kentucky Derby, an indication of its growing prominence. Louisville firms closed at 1:00 PM on Derby Day, as they still do. Among the crowd were Kentucky senator James Beck and Dame Helena Modjeska, who would soon star in the American premier of Ibsen's *A Doll's House* in Louisville.

As a local orchestra struck up "Dixie," the favorites for the Kentucky Derby, Leonard and Vera Cruz, stepped onto the track. Leonard dominated at the start while Baden-Baden got away fifth but soon rushed Leonard and charged into the lead at the finish to win by two lengths.

Baden-Baden's jockey, Willy Walker, had ridden Ten Broeck, perhaps one of the greatest horses then running, for two long-distance records against time at the Louisville Jockey Club track prior to the Derby. The records stand today. And Baden-Baden's trainer, Ed Brown, a winning rider in his youth, enjoyed great success and respect in his career and would have been a winning Derby owner had he not sold the 1898 victor, Plaudit, to John Madden.

Immediately after the race, J.T. Williams, the owner of fourth-place finisher, Vera Cruz, challenged Baden-Baden's owner, Dan Swigert, to a match race with an inviting $2,500 tag. Swigert sagely refused, saying he wouldn't tempt the gods twice.

Watching the finish from the old grandstand, Major Barak Thomas turns away as his horse, the favored Himyar, is outdistanced by Day Star. Carriages and mule-drawn trolleys surround the original judges' stand in the infield.

Policemen at the Association track on Derby Day, 1878, wore new summer uniforms and stiff-brimmed straw hats. Lemonade stands sprouted up in the infield, which was opened free to the public. The 6,000 fans took the opportunity to see firsthand the famous three-year-olds as well as politicians like General Eli H. Murray, later governor of Utah, and famous minstrel and Baptist minister, Billy Emerson, who secretly bet the winner Day Star.

Major Barak Thomas, who owned the favorite, Himyar, was the sheriff of Fayette County and a Confederate war veteran who'd returned to Kentucky to breed horses. He was an innovator in racing practices and initiated the use of numbers on saddlecloths. Fearing foul play the night before the Derby, he'd slept in Himyar's stall; however, he had to stand by helplessly on Derby Day as Himyar was bumped by every horse in the race. Day Star led from start to finish.

Day Star, bred at Ashland by John Clay, son of Henry Clay, was purchased as a yearling for $825 by T.J. Nichols, the same T.J. Nichols who had sold the 1876 winner, Vagrant, two weeks before the Derby. Day Star's career really began in his third year with the Kentucky Derby, his first major win. A grandson of Lexington, he was the third Lexington descendant to win the Derby in its short four-year history. The chestnut colt ultimately raced a total of six years both on the flat and later over fences.

Lord Murphy ✦ *May 20, 1879*

Jockey Charles Shauer on Lord Murphy, the first of three Tennessee-breds to win the Derby, poses in front of the original clubhouse built in 1875.

*L*ouisville in 1879 was recovering from the financial panic that began in 1873. The return to prosperity was evident in the double-breasted jackets and Derby bowlers of the city's well-dressed men.

There was pari-mutuel wagering at the Louisville oval, but most bettors still favored auction pools that were sold at the Galt House in downtown Louisville. The fifth Kentucky Derby was to be a contest between horses from Tennessee and Kentucky. Kentucky breds had won the first four Derbies and were generally regarded as among the finest racehorses in the world. Lord Murphy, bred in Tennessee, was the favorite. Falsetto, bred in Frankfort, Kentucky, by Hunt Reynolds and ridden by Isaac Murphy, was the prime contender. Though he finished second, he later sired three Derby winners.

The drum rolled, the red bunting fell, and General Pike and Trinidad took the lead into the first run. While pushing to the front, Lord Murphy was bumped and almost knocked out of the race. He recovered in time to charge from seventh in a field of nine and win by a length over Falsetto.

Lord Murphy was subsequently bought by Kentucky breeder James Keene and raced at America's best tracks for the remainder of his three-year-old season. At ages four and five the bay colt raced in England, but making only one start each year, he was unplaced in both races. Lord Murphy was the fourth of 52 Derby winners descended from the great sire, Lexington.

Fonso ✦ *May 18, 1880*

Robert A. Alexander, who bred Fonso, poses with the chestnut colt in front of his mansion at Woodburn Stud. He was the first man in the U.S. to make thoroughbred breeding a profession.

he sixth running of the Kentucky Derby was called the dust bowl by writers and racegoers who attended the event. The track was covered with dust several inches thick, making it nearly impossible for anyone to see the race—including the jockeys.

Alexander was a founding member of the Kentucky Association for the Improvement of the Breeds of Stock, which came into being when the Civil War changed the way of life in the South. The old, genteel manner was gone, and the great thoroughbreds could no longer be raised for sport. The refinement of the racehorse became a business.

In the days Alexander held his sales at Woodburn, business was conducted in an atmosphere quite different from today's plush pavilions: the yearlings ran free until sales time. At the sales, prospective buyers had to make themselves comfortable standing under the shade trees or sitting cross-legged on the grass.

J.S. Shawhan purchased Fonso as a yearling from Woodburn in 1878. The chestnut colt was a son of King Alfonso, the stud who replaced the great Lexington at Woodburn when he died there in 1875. Alexander had purchased Lexington for the sum of $15,000, the highest price paid up to that time for an American stallion.

One of a total of five Kentucky Derby winners produced by Woodburn, Fonso began his three-year-old career by winning the Phoenix Stakes at Lexington. His next start was the Kentucky Derby, where he broke in front of the five-horse field and stayed in the lead the entire mile-and-a-half to win over Kimball by seven lengths. Kimball's rider, Billy Lakeland, claimed foul against Fonso, but it was disallowed. Fonso started only one more time as a three-year-old in the Viley Stakes and came in second.

Hindoo ✦ May 17, 1881

The great champion in his stall with the Dwyer Brothers and trainer James Rowe, Sr.

Fans flocked to Louisville in every manner of conveyance from cart to tandem coach. The crowd fille the track grounds trying to get a glimpse of the renowned Hindoo, one of the greatest Derby champ ons of all times. He turned out to be a source of frustration to his owners, Philip and Michael Dwyer, who wer betting men and could never get a decent price on their star performer. The Dwyers, two butchers fror Brooklyn, made quite a contrast to the Wall Street types who filled the ranks of racehorse owners. A contem porary writer said: "It would not be accurate to say that the Dwyer Brothers dominated racing in their time, bu they came near it. For 30 years there was hardly a great race run in which one of their horses did not figur conspicuously." Midway through a two-year-old season in which the bay colt had won seven stakes, Hindo was purchased by the brothers.

In the seventh Kentucky Derby, each of Hindoo's five challengers took a shot at him during the course o the mile-and-a-half, but Hindoo withstood them all for an easy win. He was to go on to win 13 more stake races that year, one of them the Monmouth Sweepstakes, an uncontested walkover. He lost his first race at ag four, but came back two days later to win at a mile-and-a-quarter. Four days after that he scored at a-mile-anc an eighth. Then he took a four-day breather before tallying another win at a mile-and-a-quarter.

His last start was the Coney Island Cup, a marathon two-and-a-quarter miles. He won easily but broke dowr finishing him as a racehorse. Consequently, the Dwyers stopped entering their horses in distance trials, leadin the trend toward shorter races.

15

**The starter cracked his whip and the horses were racing. Apollo, second from
the outside, was on his way to victory in the eighth Kentucky Derby.**

The Louisville Jockey Club had expanded the seating capacity of the grandstand to nearly double its original size. It could now seat 42,000, more than any other track in the country. The Dwyer Brothers were confident of a win. Their horse Runnymeade was the favorite and Hindoo had won effortlessly for them the previous year.

Fate, however, smiled instead on Apollo's owners, Morris and Patton, and his breeder, Daniel Swigert, who had bred Hindoo. Apollo, the chestnut gelded son of Ashtead or Lever (the latter is given credit), had begun his career as a three-year-old. The grandson of Lexington took three major stakes races at three different tracks before going on to Louisville.

At the start the horses formed a ragged line across the track, as was the system then. The drummer rolled his drum and the red flag fell. Runnymeade took command and looked the easy winner until jockey Babe Hurd started his charge on Apollo one-eighth mile from the finish. Apollo caught Runnymeade a few "jumps" from the imaginary finish line and won by a half-length.

Apollo finished his three-year-old year with 10 wins in 21 starts. Then, as a four-year-old, he went on to win 14 races, nine of them in succession, out of 30 trips to the post.

In those early days, a thoroughbred was raced and raced again unmercifully, sometimes twice in a week or even every other day. In some instances, a horse was raced twice in the same day and over courses much longer than what the modern racegoer has come to expect. Long-distance trials of three and four miles were not uncommon. The thoroughbreds of the 1880s and 1890s were by necessity a stockier lot—heavier in body and legs—that had to endure so much more concussion than our fine-legged speedsters of today. The early American racehorse rarely snapped a foreleg, suffered buck shins or broke down.

Leonatus, son of Longfellow, poses with jockey Bill Donohue in the silks of co-owners Jack Chin and G.W. Morgan. In the background a gentleman rests against his penny-farthing bicycle.

The Louisville Jockey Club Course, as it was then called, was rapidly becoming the best track in the country under the supervision of its creator, Colonel M. Lewis Clark. Inspired by the 1872 Epsom Derby in England, Clark had formed the Louisville Jockey Club upon his return to the States and leased land for the track from relatives—John and Henry Churchill. With $100 from each of 320 original members, Clark built his track—a bargain at $32,000. It remained the Louisville Jockey Club Course or Louisville Race Track until 1886, when a columnist dubbed it "Churchill Downs" and the name stuck. Impartial as a presiding judge and always impeccably turned out, Colonel Clark presented an imposing figure complete with boutonniere and field glasses. A promoter first and a horseman second, he possessed only one horse, a white mare he used to pull his buggy.

Of 50 nominations for the Kentucky Derby, seven started in this, its ninth running. Leonatus, the 9 to 5 favorite, paid $14.80 and took home $3,760. (Second place was a mere $200.)

Leonatus was beaten in his only race as a two-year-old. At three he was started at Lexington, Kentucky, where he won the Blue Ribbon Stakes. His next win would put him in the pages of history. In the Derby, Leonatus caught leader Drake Carter in the first quarter and never was headed, winning by three lengths. His three-year-old season was brilliant but his career short, as he broke down in training and never ran again. His phenomenal record of ten wins and one second in 11 starts earned him $21,435, a large amount for the day, and a tidy profit for Messrs. Chinn and Morgan, who had paid a mere $5,000 for the bay colt. Leonatus' sire Longfellow, fathered another Derby winner, Riley (1890), before his death at Frank Harper's Natura Stud.

Buchanan ✦ May 16, 1884

Buchanan, the winner of the tenth Kentucky Derby. Isaac Murphy, his celebrated black jockey, also rode winners Riley (1890) and Kingman (1891).

In 1884, Louisville suffered a flood so devastating the population gave up their buggies and carts for rowboats and canoes. The wet spring did not, however, deter the 5,000 enthusiasts who showed up at the Jockey Club Track for the tenth running of the "Big Race."

Buchanan was the first horse Isaac Murphy rode to victory in the Kentucky Derby. Murphy went on to be the first jockey to win two Derbys back to back and the first jockey voted to the American Racing Hall of Fame in the Racing Museum at Saratoga Springs, a record not matched for 39 years and not bested for 57 years. He was known for his pleasing personality and was completely honest, an attribute not possessed by all riders of his day or ours. By his own records he rode 1,412 races in his career and won 628, or 44 percent. Eddie Arcaro, who rode five Derby winners himself and had a 20 percent winning average, said he doubted whether any jockey would ever come close to this.

Buchanan was temperamental and would just as soon throw a rider as carry him. Isaac Murphy had ridden him at Nashville where the colt had bolted and run off and Murphy was not overjoyed at the prospect of riding him again. But the Jockey Club judges and Colonel Clark threatened to penalize Murphy if he refused to ride.

Buchanan started badly and Bob Miles, followed by Powhattan III and the favorite, Audrain, took the lead. Murphy was undaunted. With the tenacity and courage that earned him lasting distinction, he managed to save ground on the first run, pull ahead in the stretch and win by two lengths. Isaac Murphy, known as the gentle jockey, never once used whip or spur.

Buchanan continued to race through 1886, earning a total of $13,110. His Derby win paid $20 for a $5 ticket—enough money in those pre-inflationary times to buy almost a month's worth of groceries.

**Joe Cotton poses with a well-dressed young groom in front of a
mule-drawn trolley, the main conveyance of the day.**

*L*ouisville was laying electric streetcar lines in 1885 that would in time provide direct transportation from downtown to the track. Cartoonist Fontaine Fox made the car famous naming it the "Toonerville Trolley" after it was electrified.

Joe Cotton, a chestnut son of King Alfonso, went off at even money having won six major stakes as a two-year-old and was heavily favored in the "tip" sheets. These betting guides first appeared at the Louisville Race Track in 1885 when a group of young boys offered them for sale. They proved amazingly accurate, and Joe Cotton was no exception. In seventh position, Joe Cotton made his move in the backstretch and slowly worked his way to the front. He had to be ridden to his ultimate effort to stave off the dual rush of Berson and Ten Booker, who came on like whirlwinds in the stretch.

Joe Cotton continued his winning ways, taking the largest purses in the Great Western Handicap, Coney Island Derby, Tidal Stakes, Himyar Stakes and four others in his three-year-old season. He won four additional stakes before retirement after his sixth season and a total of $29,365 earned.

A.J. Alexander of Woodford County bred five Kentucky Derby winners of which Joe Cotton was the third, yet he never owned a Derby starter. He had taken over the breeding operation upon the death of his brother, Robert, who had saved it from marauding bands of guerrillas who laid waste to farms in the South during the Civil War. Robert, fearing the loss of his farm, had advertised his great sire, Lexington, and other stallions for sale. He gave 34 horses to Harry Belland to race and sell as he saw fit. Belland earned $300,000 in purses and sales in four years and saved Woodburn from disaster. Woodburn Stud went on to flourish under A.J.'s guidance.

Owner James Ben Haggin studies the "card" as Ben Ali is cooled out. Two prosperous gentlemen look on in admiration in the casual setting of the times.

James Ben Haggin, a native Kentuckian who had made his fortune in copper and gold in California, had arrived in Louisville from the East only to find the "bookmakers" had gone on strike. Haggin informed the track officials that if no satisfactory settlement was found he would withdraw his considerable string of horses from the meeting. He let it be known in no uncertain terms that he wanted to back his own horse. The next day the bookies were on the track. However, a track official's derogatory remark was reported to him and he moved his horses out of Louisville the day after winning the Derby. It was a quarter-of-a-century before Haggin returned to Kentucky and established Elmendorf Farm with its 25 rooms and impeccable lawns. The millions from his vast holdings enabled him to make Elmendorf one of the greatest blue grass estates of the era. He became the largest commercial breeder of thoroughbreds in the country. Named for his son, Ben Ali was Haggin's pride and joy. The colt was the son of Virgil, who had previously sired the Derby winners Vagrant (1876) and Hindoo (1881).

Seven horses in the 1886 Derby field were Kentucky breds and all carried 118 pounds, the first time that weight had been assigned, with a five-pound allowance for fillies. Ben Ali was favored. At the start, Masterpiece broke in front and was followed to the first turn by Harrodsburg and Sir Joseph. At the three-quarter-mile mark Free Knight took the lead with "Snapper" Garrison in the irons, followed by Blue Wing and Ben Ali under Paul Duffy. Ben Ali and Blue Wing battled neck and neck through the stretch until Ben Ali pulled ahead to win by a half-length, setting a new Derby record. In his three-year-old campaign, Ben Ali took top honors in seven out of 12 starts.

Jockey Isaac Lewis sits astride Montrose. The bay colt was bred by Colonel Milton Young, of Ohio, who purchased the famous McGrathiana Stud upon the death of Price McGrath. In the background, a mule-drawn water wagon wends its way up the dirt road.

*J*ames Ben Haggin, millionaire horseman and speculator, had withdrawn his stable from the last year's meeting a day after winning the Derby with Ben Ali. Haggin shunned Louisville, including the Derby, and raced instead in the East and in California. Without the Haggin entries, the field was one of the smallest ever started in a Kentucky Derby and judged by horsemen of the day as inferior to years past.

However, the crowd never weakened in its enthusiasm. They were there for a good time and to be "on the winner." The stage was being set for the fashion shows of the future. The well-dressed man sported a straw Conductor, Breakman or Buckner "boater," while the more affluent wore the world-renowned Knox.

As the seven candidates paraded before the stands, the favorite, Banburg, was wildly cheered. Montrose received only a polite reception, mostly by the Ohioans who had backed him. Starter Billy Cheatham got the field away without incident. Jacobin led at the first but was soon overtaken by Montrose. The favorite challenged but Montrose outran him in the backstretch. Jim Gore moved up quickly in the final dash, but Montrose held on and won easily. The 13 Kentucky Derby winner was the second of the Matchem bloodline to triumph at the Derby after Baden-Baden (1877).

Macbeth II ✦ May 14, 1888

Macbeth II on the backstretch with young George Covington up. In the infield, fans watch from a farm wagon and a mule-drawn streetcar—public transportation of the day.

Fourteen thousand fans braved a cold, windy day to see the Kentucky Derby. The favorite was Gallifet and coupled with Alexandria made up the entry from Melbourne Stable. But the brown gelding, Macbeth II, the son of Macduff, carrying the orange and black silks of that Chicago Stable, was about to take the silver punch bowl—the first time a Derby winner would carry a stable's colors. The year of 1888 was also the inaugural of the Belmont Futurity in New York, with its rich purse of $40,900.

As the horses lined up for the Derby, a motion from the flagman sent them off early. The second start was clean and The Chevalier jumped into the lead. He was soon overtaken by Gallifet, who led the pack until well into the homestretch when Macbeth II with young George Covington bolted to the front and took the race by a length.

The first race on the program this Derby Day had been a rerun. The horses had started from the half-mile pole instead of the intended five-eighths pole, and rather than postpone the race to a later date, the officials simply ran the tired horses again—this time an eighth of a mile longer!

Macbeth II won $22,170 and was the third gelding to win the Derby; not another racehorse would do so until Old Rosebud in 1914.

And no other Derby winner until then would go on to race as much as Macbeth II did in his lifetime—106 starts in seven seasons of which 25 were wins.

Spokane ✦ *May 9, 1889*

A victory portrait of Spokane done in the style of the period.

The year 1889 saw the first $2 ticket sold. It was also the last year auction pools would be allowed; they were discontinued until Churchill Downs president Matt Winn reinstated them in 1908. This was also the year Louisville got its first electric streetcar. The last mule-drawn trolley would leave the streets in 1901.

Sammy Barnes, the crack lightweight, was chosen to ride Proctor Knott, but Barnes was too small to control the big favorite. Spokane, bred in Illinois, foaled in Montana and trained in Tennessee, had raced well as a two year-old but not as well as Proctor Knott. A chestnut colt by Hyder Ali and a descendant of Lexington, Spokane' odds were 10 to 1. Proctor Knott broke away from the start twice, bolting each time a good eighth-of-a-mile down the track. Nearly unseating his rider with a series of spectacular lunges, he nevertheless broke with the field on the third try and shot to an early lead, which he opened to five lengths as they rounded the clubhouse turn. Entering the far turn, jockey Tom Kiley sent Spokane skimming along the rail past Once Again and pulled almost even with Proctor Knott with a quarter-mile left to run. It became a desperate match race: at the one eighth pole, just when he appeared to have it won, Proctor Knott bolted for the outer rail, and by the time "Pike" Barnes had straightened his colt, Spokane had gained a slim lead, which he managed to hold despite Proctor Knott's last desperate drive.

The margin of victory was a nose, and the crowd remained convinced that Proctor Knott was the better horse with the exception of Frank James, Jesse's brother, who had $5,000 on Spokane. A few days later, Spokane came back to prove his class with another game score over his highly touted rival in the Clark Stakes at one and one-quarter miles.

MAY 9, 1885

© Bryant '82

Riley ✦ May 14, 1890

Owner-trainer "Big Ed" Corrigan proudly leads his winner with jockey Isaac Murphy before an admiring group including Billy Lakeland. The ornate original grandstand is in the background with its twin towers.

A downpour kept the crowd on the small side at the 16th Derby even though the city had closed the pool halls for the duration of the meet to encourage track attendance. Six starters faced the flag, one of the smallest fields to date, with Robespierre going off as the even-money favorite. That colt put on a wild display parading to the post, convincing even more bettors that this was the beast to back. The start was good and the horses stayed tightly bunched as they passed the stands for the first time. Riley trailed the pack. Halfway down the backstretch Isaac Murphy gave Riley his head, and as they entered the far turn Riley was in front by two lengths, an advantage he maintained at the wire. He became the winner of the first of many rain-soaked Derbies.

Riley, a bay colt by Longfellow, was the second of three Derby winners for Isaac Murphy, the jockey who many believed had a special communication with horses. Murphy would win the Derby the following year on Kingman, and Riley's sire, Longfellow, had already produced the 1883 Derby winner, Leonatus—whose victory had also come over a wet track.

A few days later, as trainers thought nothing then of running a horse twice in one week, Riley was back on the track for the Clark Stakes, which he also won. Of his 64 career starts, Riley won 30, and despite starting 2 times in his three-year-old year and 15 in his four-year-old year, he continued to race without breaking down until his retirement in 1894, his seventh year. His career earnings total was $43,430.

33

Isaac Murphy on Kingman in the winner's circle with
Jacobin Stable co-owner, Kinzea Stone.

*L*ouisville's Union Station was completed in 1891. For the next 50 years the station would be a famous meeting place for arriving Derby guests.

On that second Saturday in May, the infield was so congested that the starter needed a police escort to clear a path to the half-mile pole where the mile-and-a-half classic would begin. "Ike" Murphy rode Kingman, who ran the slowest Derby ever. Without each other's knowledge, the owners and trainers of each of the four-horse field—one of the smallest in Derby history—instructed their riders to lay back for most of the race, then charge at the finish. A quarter-mile from home, all four were across the track, nose-to-nose, as if in a cavalry charge. Then Balgowan made his move and Murphy took off after him. Kingman won by a half-length.

Kingman had been bred in Tennessee by A.C. Franklin and was the second Derby winner to hail from that state, the first being Lord Murphy in 1879. The brown colt raced only two years, earning nearly $20,000 in 28 starts, a large amount for the day.

Kingman was Isaac Murphy's third Derby victory. He'd begun his riding career in 1874, a year before the first Kentucky Derby, at the age of 14. He weighed only 70 pounds and went to work for the stable of Williams and Owings. At the time many of the jockeys were black, as they were the only ones who handled the horses and knew and rode them best. Fifteen of the first 28 Derbies were won by black jockeys. As the sport became more lucrative, white jockeys took over.

Just prior to his death in 1896, Murphy was quoted as saying, "I am as proud of my calling as I am of my record, and I believe my life will be recorded as a success, although the reputation I enjoy was earned in the stable and the saddle."

Azra, the bay colt with young jockey Alonzo Clayton, catches Huron at the wire in the 18th running. The original judges' stand is in the background.

The 1892 Kentucky Derby, with only three starters, was the smallest field to date. Originally, owner George Long—also the breeder of Derby winners Manuel (1899) and Sir Huon (1906)—planned to have stablemate Bashford run with Azra. However, when rain left the course heavy, trainer John Morris decided to scratch Bashford. The two horses had raced brilliantly during 1891 and were considered the best two-year-olds of that season.

Jockey Britton on Huron tried to set a pace that would kill Azra and the third entry, Phil Dwyer. Swinging the big bay colt to the rail, he drew away from Azra, who Clayton held well in hand, and gradually increased his lead by five lengths. Phil Dwyer was held in reserve by Jockey Overton. Nearing the first quarter they all ran wide at the turn seeking drier ground. Down the backstretch, Huron easily ran two lengths in the lead. Huron looked like the winner as the crowd cheered. As they neared the last quarter, Azra gained on Huron, forging to the front. They reached the stretch on even terms. The stands swelled with excitement. By the eighth pole, Huron had pulled a neck ahead of Azra, but as they approached the finish Azra made another rush and caught Huron to win by a nose. The 10,000 in attendance witnessed this fine test of courage and cheered winner and loser alike.

Following his Derby triumph, Azra won the Clark Stakes and left Churchill Downs for the East where he won the Travers Stakes at Saratoga and placed frequently in other races. Although successful, Azra's career was woefully short: One morning, when trainer Morris had invited a number of friends to the barn to inspect his string and Azra had been paraded for the guests, his groom rushed back to Morris with the news that the great horse was "down" in his stall. The winner of the 1892 Kentucky Derby was dead at the age of three.

Lookout ♦ *May 10, 1893*

Described in a Louisville paper a day after his win as splendidly muscled with a better set of legs seldom placed under a thoroughbred, the rich golden chestnut poses with his groom. Trainer William McDaniel is in the background.

Drenched by rain the day and night before, the track was wet but fast by race time. The sun came out in the morning and 30,000 racing enthusiasts headed for the "Downs." This year, for the first time, women were allowed to place their own wagers.

More horses had shown up for this meeting than any other in the track's history, and temporary stabling had been set up in an old hay barn and every other available shed as they poured in by the trainload from as far away as Washington, D.C. "Railbirds" were in despair. Although they'd been able to clock the final pre-Derby workouts of nearly all the entries, Plutus had eluded them and it was confusing their bookmaking. If trainer Morris had given the Bashford Manor colt a final breeze it must have been in the dark.

Among the entries, there were three outstanding horses that had done well on a wet track: Boundless in the Arkansas Derby, Lookout at Memphis, and Linger in the Distillers Stakes at Lexington. In addition, Buck McCann would benefit from his sire's talent for the slop, his sire having been the 1884 winner, Buchanan.

Lookout's jockey, Ed Kunze, had received his instructions from trainer William McDaniel to "kill 'em," and from the time the crimson bunting fell, Lookout dominated. With not a spot of mud on his golden coat, he galloped past the finish pole untouched by steel or whip, leaving in his wake, four lengths back, the five weary stragglers. It had been a fine field, with each horse worthy of a Derby appearance, but they'd been made to look unfit by the excellence of Lookout. It had been a June day in 1886 when Troubadour, Lookout's sire, had triumphed in much the same way at the Sheepshead Bay Racecourse.

**Trainer Eugene Leigh tacks up the eventual winner as jockey
Frank Goodal looks on in controlled anticipation.**

In 1894 a 24-year-old native Louisvillian, Joseph D. Valdez, saw what would be his most famous architectural creation erected at Churchill Downs. The new grandstand with its twin spires would face the east, a welcome improvement for racegoers who formerly had to stare into the sun throughout an afternoon's racing.

Small fields had plagued the Derby since Haggin had walked out with his string of top horses after his 1886 Derby win with Ben Ali. Many Eastern stables had boycotted the Downs in sympathy. Also, as racing had become increasingly more a business than a sport, owners were reluctant to run their best colts the grueling one-and-a-half-mile distance so early in the season. These factors, plus the financial instability of the track, contributed to the lightness of this field—only five started. By the end of the year, the Clark regime had fallen, replaced by the New Louisville Jockey Club, which put $100,000 into track improvements, including the new grandstand; however, the current Derby distance of one-and-a-quarter miles would not be instituted until 1896.

Despite the perfect weather and record crowd, the 20th Kentucky Derby was not one of the most memorable. All five starters carried the same impost—122 pounds—perhaps one cause for the unspectacular event. The winner was decided before the race was half over. Chant led at the half-mile by two lengths and loped past the wire with the field strung out for 40 lengths behind him. With a time of 2:41, it was the slowest Derby with the exception of Riley in 1890. The fastest had been Lord Murphy in 1879.

Fate had smiled on jockey Goodale by giving him the most satisfying win a jockey could earn only to take him from the track forever in a race two days after his Derby triumph. Goodale was killed in the saddle when his mount stumbled and fell.

Halma ✦ *May 6, 1895*

Jockey James "Soup" Perkins steadies Halma. Perkins in Byron McClelland's silks (lower left, inset).

In the last three Derbies a total of only 14 horses had gone to the post and the track was losing money. Colonel Clark's Louisville Jockey Club had given way to the New Louisville Jockey Club, a group of professional gamblers. They realized that some drastic improvements had to be made and had funded the new grandstand and many other refurbishments. Unfortunately, the Derby distance of one-and-a-half-miles was not shortened.

The unpopular distance resulted in only four starters for the 21st Derby: Halma with Perkins; Basso with Martin; Laureate with Clayton; and Curator with Overton. Despite the small field, the opening of the new track was a huge success, drawing over 20,000.

Halma had the striking attributes of his sire, Hanover, with massive shoulders and perfect legs, a deep chest and flowing action. A cheer swelled from the crowd as the 16-year-old "Soup" Perkins, in McClelland's green and orange colors, rode from the paddock.

The track was fast and the race was decided early. Little "Soup" had wrapped the reins around his arms up to his elbows hoping to hold Halma, who charged to the front in spite of him and pulled away from the field. As they neared the grandstand for the first time he had opened his lead to a length. Laureate held on, but Curator "stopped" with comical quickness. Halma widened his lead to two lengths at the mile, and still under Soup's tight wraps, appeared to be out for an exercise gallop. He romped under the wire three lengths ahead of his nearest pursuer.

James Perkins is still the youngest jockey to win the Derby. Only 18-year-old Steve Cauthen on Affirmed came close in 1978. The year of Halma's Derby saw the retirement of the great Isaac Murphy, known to all as Honest Ike.

**Ben Brush breathes heavily as jockey Willie Simms unsaddles him
after their victory in the 22nd Derby.**

It was the beginning of a new era. Declaring the mile-and-a-half distance too grueling a test, the new management shortened the race to the mile-and-a-quarter, which it remains today. The new length was an immediate success with the horsemen as a record 171 horses were nominated that year, although only 8 started. Among the entrants was the Eastern "Wonder Horse," Ben Brush, making a rare Southern appearance.

At the start, Semper Ego and Ben Brush took an early lead. Then Ben Brush stumbled but recovered and going into the turn past the stands the horses were tightly bunched. Suddenly, like a thunderbolt, First Mate broke from the pack and was two lengths on top by the backstretch with the favorite, Ben Brush, coasting in fourth place. Ben Brush made his move along with Ben Eder and by the top of the stretch it was a four-horse race with First Mate losing ground and Semper Ego straining to keep pace. With Ben Eder on his flank, Ben Brush started to weaken, but Simms dug in his spurs and they reached the finish nose-to-nose, with the big Eastern horse winning by inches. Ben Brush triumphed but many considered Ben Eder the better horse.

Ben Brush was the leading sire of 1909 when his sons and daughters accumulated $75,143 in purse money. His great-granddaughters produced Derby winners Bubbling Over, War Admiral and Whirlaway. Of his sons, Broomstick sired Meridian (1911 Derby) and Regret, the first filly to take the honors in 1915.

The great jockey Isaac Murphy had fallen victim to the rigors of losing up to 40 pounds each time racing season came around, compounded by the doses of champagne he drank to keep going. With his resistance at an all-time low, he died of pneumonia at the age of 35. His untimely death came one year after his retirement and shocked the racing world of 1896. Over 500 people, as many black as white, attended his funeral. The $30,000 he left to his wife was decimated by debts and she died childless in a pauper's grave. Only a simple wooden cross marked his grave which was soon obscured by weeds and grass. It was eventually discovered and Murphy's remains were moved to a Lexington park where he was reburied near the grave of Man o' War.

45

The drummer has rolled his drum, the starter's gun has gone off and the assistant starters slash at the field with their whips.

Most of the smart money had been on the favorite, Ornament, in the pools that were still operated in downtown Louisville despite much grumbling from the bookmakers. As the drizzle started Tuesday morning, however, those in the Typhoon II camp took heart as he had proven to have a liking for the slop. "Buttons" Garner, Fred Taral's replacement on Typhoon II, was so confident that he had advised his cohorts to put their money on his horse.

Twenty thousand were treated to a contest that was in doubt up until the end. Typhoon II, bred and owned in the sister state of Tennessee, had plunged and wheeled and after six minutes at the start took the lead immediately. Left at the post and caught in the heavy going, Ornament gamely tried to close in on the leader, who led from pole to pole with such a burst of speed that not one of the nation's best three-year-olds could catch the chestnut colt. Ornament ran a suspiciously timed race. He came flying from behind but could do no better than reach Typhoon II's saddlecloth in a last desperate surge at the finish line.

Charlie Patterson, the trainer and part-owner of Ornament, was found later in his barn whittling casually on a railing as his horse was cooled out. Apparently unperturbed by the upset, he felt it had happened before and it would probably happen again. But "Buttons" Garner was jubilant. Taking great whiffs of his roses between short breaths as he stepped off the scales, he said he had known no horse could touch them except Ornament and that when Alonzo Clayton had finally set sail for Typhoon at the final eighth, "Buttons" simply had to lean forward a little and speak to his horse.

Plaudit ✦ *May 4, 1898*

In the paddock, Plaudit's owner, John Madden (in straw hat), plans his strategy with jockey Willie Simms.

The morning of the Derby had been wet and gloomy and the expected record crowd never materialized despite clearing skies in the afternoon. Plaudit, a son of Himyar, who had been deprived of victory 20 year earlier by Day Star and a plot to defeat him, would this day vindicate his sire's loss. The Kentucky Derby wa the brown colt's first start as a three-year-old. His owner/trainer, John Madden, would be America's leading breeder from 1912 until 1927 and the first breeder to produce a Triple Crown winner (Sir Barton), yet no vic tor in the Derby would ever carry his colors after Plaudit.

The race was a masterpiece of riding by jockey Willie Simms. When the flag fell, Lieber Karl shot to the fron with Han d'Or and Isabey in hot pursuit. Plaudit was last, running easily. On the backstretch, he moved or Lieber Karl leaving Han d'Or and Isabey in the dust. At the top of the stretch, Plaudit caught Lieber Karl. Plaudi kept stride with the big colt and moved to take over the lead in the stretch. The crowd went wild as both hors es fought a desperate duel for a short distance. Then Plaudit was in front, gradually drawing away, and crossed the finish first by a neck.

It was the second Derby win in three years for Willie Simms. He was the first jockey ever to ride "short although that credit has been awarded to the English jockey Tod Sloan. Actually, Simms rode short in England one year before Sloan.

Manuel ✦ May 4, 1899

Although the upright style of jockeys makes them appear to be out for a canter, this is a hard-fought battle with Manuel and Fred Taral (inset) besting His Lordship at the top of the stretch.

Starting with Manuel in 1899 and ending with Donerail in 1913, the Derby was characterized by mediocrity. The trend started with Typhoon II's win in 1897 when the favorite, Ornament, received a suspicious ride, and coupled with the change in management and local opposition to gambling the Derby became a local affair riding on its reputation. Colonel M. Lewis Clark, the father of Churchill Downs and the Derby, sadly ended his life by his own hand two weeks before the 25th running.

Since the Derby's inception in 1875, 24 winners and over 180 hopeful three-year-olds had passed under the wire. And although the entries were slim (with only five horses parading to the post), the crowd was large and the racing of high quality.

True to form, Manuel sprang to the front as the bunting fell. Jockey Fred Taral, saving the bay colt, pulled back behind His Lordship and Fontainebleu, and as the field passed the stands for the first time, Taral had Manuel comfortably in third place. Keeping his mount within striking distance, Taral waited for the right moment and sent him bolting at the half-mile. Manuel shot to the lead and was an easy victor by the home stretch. He crossed the finish a full two lengths to the good of Corsini. Corsini, tired from his long trip from the Pacific Coast, responded gamely to Burns' whip but couldn't catch the Dutchman from New York who spurred Manuel on to insure his win. Manuel was never fully extended.

Although it was a day of triumph for Manuel, many favorite sons mourned the passing of Colonel Clark and reflected on the good old days of the Louisville Jockey Club when Clark ruled with an iron fist. Not only had he been an accomplished organizer and leader, but a respected track judge as well. Fair to a fault, no discrepancy eluded his attention and no favors were granted.

Lieutenant Gibson ✦ May 3, 1900

Jockey Jimmy Boland casually poses with Lieutenant Gibson in front of Churchill Downs president W.F. Schulte's coach-and-four.

The air was clear and the track fast—a perfect day for the swiftest Derby ever. The 26th Derby was contested before a record crowd of 30,000 with a larger field than recent years.

An experimental rubber barrier snapped against the infield rail and a massive roar went up from the crowd as the race started. Lieutenant Gibson broke with His Excellency and Kentucky Farmer. The three horses ran as if chained together and created a classic picture for the tabloids as they charged past the stands through a cloud of dust. At the first turn the race took on a different look with Lieutenant Gibson first and the rest of the field second. Almost without effort Lieutenant Gibson had swept into the lead, which he never relinquished. It was reported that the great colt never extended himself yet he bested Ben Brush's time for the inaugural run over the one-and-a-quarter miles by $1^2/_5$ seconds. Champion three-year-olds all, the balance of the field had been made to look like a bunch of "platers." Lieutenant Gibson's record would stand for 11 years when Meridian would cover the distance in 2:05. Charles Head Smith, Lieutenant Gibson's owner, didn't have a dime on his horse, yet was pleased with the win not only for himself but for the entire Board of Trade of Chicago, which had put a considerable amount of dimes on Lieutenant Gibson.

It was preferable to have your horse finish in the clear in those days, as the dust was so thick a close finish was nearly unjudgeable.

His Eminence strikes a formal pose, as though taking his cue from owner F.B. VanMeter who stands next to the latest in "two-wheelers."

*D*espite record crowds for the 27th Derby and a Derby record set the year before, the event was still in danger for its life. The great Eastern Stables continued to shun it, and the Downs was still plagued by internal management problems and financial difficulties.

Another small field, but five of the country's best, went to the post, including His Eminence, with Jimmy Winkfield making his second Derby appearance (he placed third the year before on Thrive) and jockey Jim Boland, the 1901 winner, on Driscoll. Sannazarro, billed earlier as the dark horse, would go off at better odds of 4 to 1. Alard Scheck was favored at 7 to 10. The top three horses had all worked speedily during their pre-Derby "blowouts" before an early morning crowd of 500, who saw His Eminence turn in the best time. The track was in its fastest condition ever and many expected records to be shattered left and right. The evening before the race, Jimmy Boland took himself out for a run with pugilist Jack McClelland in the hopes of shedding extra poundage, yet returned still 3½ pounds overweight, which may have figured in the results.

"They're off!" and before 50 yards had slid under his hooves, His Eminence had taken over the lead. Winkfield was riding beautifully as he passed the half-mile in 51 seconds. He had the race won and he knew it. Meanwhile, Alard Scheck—the odds-on favorite—was bringing up the rear. As His Eminence crossed under the wire, Alard Scheck committed a racing sin. Instead of responding to his rider's urgings, he sulked and finished five lengths behind the last horse. Jimmy Boland on Driscoll finished third. This was the first of two winning performances in the saddle over a Derby course for black jockey Jimmy Winkfield. The next would come with Alan-a-Dale the following year.

Alan-a-Dale ✦ May 3, 1902

Jimmy Winkfield, dapper in sportcoat, slacks and cap, gives Alan-a-Dale a pre-Derby workout. Soulful and proud, he stares out at us from the past (inset).

The first automobile coughed down the boulevard and the electrification of the city's mule-cars wa completed. Churchill Downs, however, was not prospering. The Derby was still drawing only average size fields. Later in the year Colonel Matt Winn, a Louisville tailor with no horseracing experience, would forn a group of buyers to take over the financially ailing track for a mere $40,000.

Alan-a-Dale, a chestnut son of Halma, the 1895 winner, was owned by Major T.C. McDowell, a great-grand son of Henry Clay, Kentucky's most popular statesman. He bred and trained the winner and was the only mar to accomplish this beside T.P. Hayes with his Donerail in 1913.

The second jockey to win two Derbies back to back after Isaac Murphy, Winkfield had made his riding debu in Chicago in a rather spectacular fashion. Breaking on the outside, he cut off three horses in his rush to the inside rail and all four went down. Winkfield was ruled off for a year only to win his first time back. He hold the best winning average for the Derby—two wins, one second and a third in only four attempts.

He rode one of his best races ever on Alan-a-Dale. McDowell had given jockey Nat Turner first choice of hi two Derby hopefuls and Winkfield, who exercised them both and knew that Alan-a-Dale was the faster, hel that horse back in workouts prior to Turner's visit. Turner picked The Rival. Alan-a-Dale, however, was so "bad legged" he had to be trained in a driving cart.

The Rival was first to take the lead but soon surrendered it to Alan-a-Dale in the first eighth. Alan-a-Dal opened his lead to four lengths, but going into the homestretch went noticeably lame. As he started to bobble Winkfield held him together and at the same time pushed Inventor, who had come up on the outside, farthe out into the deep sand. Alan-a-Dale won by a nose. This was the first start as a three-year-old for this gam young horse and one that cost him dearly. He did not start again until his fourth season.

Judge Himes ✦ May 2, 1903

Triple portrait of trainer J.P. Mayberry and jockey Hal Booker in front of Judge Himes.

*E*arly was the crowd's favorite. They could be forgiven for overlooking Judge Himes. He had managed to get to the wire first in only one of his ten starts as a two-year-old and failed to impress at three. But the chestnut colt was brought up to the classic by J.P. Mayberry, a trainer whose horses made up in conditioning what they lacked in class. Actually, Judge Himes should have looked like a good bet. He was owned by Charles R. Ellison, the "Blond Plunger," known to be one of the heaviest bettors in the country.

As it turned out, Judge Himes may have owed his win to a jockey—not his own, Hal Booker, but to Jimmy Winkfield on the favorite, Early. Winkfield, having won the last two Derbies, had set his sights on beating Isaac Murphy's record of three wins with two back-to-back. Winkfield wanted three back-to-back. In his eagerness, he urged Early to run too soon, and when the sore-heeled Judge Himes came up on the inside, Early had nothing left.

Winkfield never forgot his faux pas. In telling the story later at his training stable in Maisons-Lafitte, France, he admitted he thought of fouling Judge Himes a little. Winkfield was a big favorite and probably would not have been disqualified. This opportunistic attitude got him into a bit of trouble with John Madden, and was one of the reasons that Wink ended up riding in Russia. "I was tops in Russia," he said.

Elwood ✦ May 2, 1904

Frankie Prior on Elwood after their win is recorded for posterity by early movie cameras, that filmed the Derby for turn-of-the-century newsreels.

In 1904 Elwood's sire was earning his oats pulling a plow—one indication why Elwood's victory came at the longest odds to date. Being a Missouri bred didn't endear him to the bettors at the 30th running of the Kentucky classic either.

The bay colt's record as a two-year-old was dreadful but he had put in a few fair tries at three, including second in the California Derby. After arriving in Louisville, he was honed to razor sharpness by C.E. Durnell husband of the horse's owner. Elwood was not only the first Derby winner owned by a woman, he was the first bred by a woman, Mrs. J.B. Prather.

In the Derby, Elwood was piloted by Frankie Prior, a California farm boy. He was unknown in Louisville but had performed impressively on the West Coast. Prior rated his homely colt patiently as the small field of five moved through the first mile. With a quarter-of-a-mile to go he was still dead last. Then Prior "got after" Elwood and they glided by the fading pacesetter with ease, arriving at the wire a half-length ahead of the favorite, Ed Tierney. This Derby win was to be the highlight of the Missouri invader's career. His only victory at four came in a curiosity event at New York's Brighton Beach Racetrack—a race restricted to jockeys who had never won.

C.E. "Boots" Durnell was not present when Elwood took the roses. He had not wanted to run a horse he didn't think had a prayer of winning. His wife, the owner, disagreed, and when she won the argument Durnell boycotted the whole affair and another trainer was asked to saddle Elwood in the paddock at Churchill Downs.

Agile ♦ *May 10, 1905*

Trainer Robert Tucker holds Agile as jockey Jack Martin loosens his girth after the 31st Kentucky Derby. The new stands and clubhouse turn are on the right. The old bandshell where summer evening concerts are held is on the left.

Agile's owner, S.S. Brown, maintained a steel mill in Pittsburgh and a fleet of riverboats that were used to haul coal and ore to it. As the operator of this fleet he dubbed himself "Captain."

Robert Tucker, as well known for his squinty eyes and handlebar moustache as for his talent as a trainer, was at the zenith of his career in 1905. The delicate-featured Jack Martin was a tough and clever jockey despite his "pretty boy" looks.

Nobody was out of the money in the 1905 Derby because only three horses had entered the contest. It was the smallest field ever with the exception of Azra's race in 1892. The competition was really only between Agile and Ram's Horn. Agile, the son of Sir Dixon and Alpena, was given the unbelievably short odds of 33¢ on the dollar.

The bugle called the three contenders from the paddock. As if he knew he was the favorite and sure winner, Agile shot under the flying web barrier and took the lead immediately. He never relinquished it, despite a bid in the stretch from Ram's Horn, and galloped under the wire. Jack Martin later stated that his horse would have won even if the track were powder-dry and not the heavy going of this race. Lucien Lyne, Ram's Horn's jockey, agreed. D. Austin, who rode Layson, and finished 20 lengths behind Ram's Horn, refused to talk. As they passed the finish, Martin was restraining Agile.

Sir Huon with jockey Roscoe Troxler painted in the English style of the period. A pair of grays pulls a gentleman's daycart toward the Derby champion.

The 32nd running of the Louisville classic shaped up as a battle of the sexes. Sir Huon won this scrimmage, outlasting the game filly, Lady Navarre. The consensus of the day was that, game though she was, a filly just could not stand up to the rigors of the Derby.

Sir Huon had been bred in the Bluegrass State by George J. Long, an industrialist and sportsman who disliked commercialism and believed in sport for sport's sake. Further, the Kentucky Derby was in Sir Huon's blood—he was the third winner sired by Falsetto. Chant and His Eminence preceded him. Sir Huon won four out of nine starts in his first year, but came up to the Derby without a prep race. The results proved he didn't need it.

Superstition was the villain that caused Sir Huon to go off at overwhelming odds in his favor. The local paper had run a pre-Derby story with a picture that showed a number five horse clearly visible. That was Sir Huon's number and he evidently picked up a good deal of "action" from the hunch players. Laying second in the early going, he got a neck in front at the mile pole and stretched his advantage to two lengths at the wire. Lady Navarre overcame interference and fought valiantly in the stretch but could not get any closer to him. Jockey Roscoe Troxler said, "I felt confident of winning. I could feel the big colt was full of run under me." He claimed that toward the end, Sir Huon was only cantering. Lady Navarre's defeat would be vindicated in 1915 when Harry Payne Whitney's filly, Regret, would be the first horse of the feminine gender to wear the blanket of roses.

Pink Star ✦ *May 6, 1907*

Andy Minder has removed his boots and saddle to pose bareback on the bald-faced Pink Star.

*M*rs. Nicholas Longworth, the former Alice Roosevelt, was the center of attraction at this 33rd running until the horses stepped onto the mud-spattered track. Then all those crowding in the stands and tho watching from tree tops on the "outside" strained to see the field. Tom Hayes' colt, Red Gauntlet, was the ove whelming favorite with odds of 3 to 2 over Ovelando at 3 to 1. But Pink Star's owner, J. Hal Woodford fro Versailles, Kentucky, remained confident. He'd seen his horse lose a race or two, yet sensed that Pink Star ha enough strength in reserve to pull this one out of the hat.

As noted by the few who bet on him at 15 to 1, Pink Star was the very image of his sire, Pink Coat, who s the record for seven-eighths-of-a-mile at Churchill Downs in 1900. Pink Star was also the grandson of the 188 winner, Leonatus, and could trace his lineage back to Leamington, who sired the first Kentucky Derby winne Aristides.

Jockey Minder rode an intelligent race, restraining the fleet bay colt in the early stages. He trailed far bac for the first three-quarters and, gradually moving up through the far turn, straightened out for the stretch ar came on with a rush that wore the leaders down. He won "going away." Little Andy Minder, whose career ha been marred by bad luck and injury at Churchill Downs, was the happiest boy in the world when own Woodford gave him $500 for his great ride, performed down to the letter of Woodford's instructions.

Trainer J W. Hall poses stoically with Arthur Pickens on Stone Street for their victory portrait with the rose blanket. "Movietone News" cameras recorded the event.

Colonel Matt J. Winn, the chairman of Churchill Downs, got the bad news a few days before the Derby was to be run: bookmaking was made illegal and that law was to be enforced at Churchill Downs beginning with its spring opener, the Derby of 1908. But the crafty colonel recalled the old pari-mutuel machines used at the track back in the 1880s. There were still a few gathering dust in storage that were serviceable, and through a flurry of telegrams he located a few more from as far away as New York. So that year, instead of bookmakers in the betting shed there were eleven pari-mutuel machines, seven for win bets and two each for place and show.

Both bettors and the machine operators were unfamiliar with the new system, which created long, slow-moving lines. Many bettors found that they actually bought place or show tickets when they had wanted to back a winner on the nose. Some profited from their mistakes, but not if they had wanted to bet Stone Street to win. He paid $123.60 for every $5.00 bet.

The long shot had not been impressive coming up to the Derby, but on Derby Day the track came up heavy with mud. Stone Street's only decent race had been over that kind of track. Nineteen-year-old jockey Arthur Pickens felt the race was his when he found himself in second place after the first quarter-mile. At the top of the stretch Stone Street had a neck in front and increased the margin to three lengths at the finish.

The Kentucky Derby was Stone Street's first, last and only stakes win, and, at 2:15⅓, the slowest Derby ever run at one-and-a-quarter miles. Kingman recorded the slowest over the one-and-a-half-mile-long course with a time of 2:52¼ in 1891.

Vincent Powers exercises Wintergreen under the admiring gaze of a group of dandies of the period. Note the "modern" stirrup length.

*P*olitician-turfman J.B. "Rome" Respess, who owned Wintergreen, had generously contributed to various racetracks and desired his crowning gift to be a Derby winner. He spared no expense on his beautiful bay colt by Dick Welles. When Wintergreen was only a few weeks old, Respess had prophesied, "This one will be the winner of the Derby in 1909," and he did all that was necessary to achieve that end.

Although his only stakes placing up to the Derby was a meager third in the Hurricane Stakes, Wintergreen had won five of his starts as a two-year-old and had the additional advantage of guidance from a leading jockey of the day, Vincent Powers, who would later succeed as a trainer as well. Miami, a strong but unpredictable colt, simply could not compete with the popular favorite, though some doubted Wintergreen could go the distance and expected him to falter near the end. They were unaware that the blood of the great sires Virgil and Herod would help him stay the course.

It had rained the morning of the 35th running but the track was in good shape. Going off at $1.96 to the dollar, Wintergreen was the obvious winner right from the start where he was bumped by Dr. Barkley but recovered instantly and took the lead. Then with the race well in hand and Miami hanging on behind him, Wintergreen faltered at the eighth pole. A muffled sigh went up from the crowd. Vincent Powers lashed at the handsome colt mercilessly. He leaped ahead like a wounded deer and came on through the corridor of sound, past the forest of waving canes and umbrellas and the thousands cheering his name to the wire.

An historical montage: Robert Herbert poses bareback and awkwardly clutches his bouquet of roses astride the 1910 winner, Donau. In the background, the first plane to fly in the state of Kentucky prepares for takeoff from the infield at Churchill Downs.

*A*dmission to the infield at the Downs was free at the 1910 running and thousands poured in from every state. The announcer's voice, amplified by a primitive microphone, was barely audible above the roar of the crowd and there was some confusion as to which horse had drawn what track position.

Donau's owner, William Gerst, was one of 20 million immigrants who had come to the "the land of milk and honey" since 1821. He had spent his childhood in Germany and built a lucrative brewery business in the United States. The name, Donau, means Danube in German.

Donau, whose short odds in this race were 1.65 to the dollar, raced more times than any other Derby winner. He had won five of his ten outings as a two-year-old and eventually won 30 of his 111 starts in a four-year career. When the barrier flew up and the assistant starters' whips cracked like rifle fire, Donau went to the lead immediately and held on to it until the stretch where he tired but gamely staved off the last bids of Joe Morris, Fighting Bob and Boola Boola. It was a four-horse race down to the wire with 40,000 screaming fans urging on their favorite.

Meridian, as a six-year-old, poses in a field at the end of his career.
His tail is short, in the style of the era.

*M*eridian, the son of Broomstick, who held the world record for one-and-a-half miles and also sired Halma, the 1895 Derby winner, won the Derby under questionable circumstances. Meridian led from "wire to wire" in the 1911 Derby, but the favorite, Governor Gray, was held back too far and for too long in the first half of the race. When he was allowed his head, he came on gamely but Meridian had enough in reserve to hold off the challenge.

After the race, Captain James T. Williams, one of the co-owners of Governor Gray, accused jockey Roscoe Troxler of deliberately giving his horse an inadequate ride. The imbroglio became even messier when it was reported that a Chicago bookmaker, Charley Ellis, had given Troxler a sum of money after the race. The 65-year-old Williams apparently "attacked" Ellis near the Churchill Downs paddock and knocked off his hat with his cane. During the subsequent investigation, Ellis claimed he only loaned Troxler a few dollars. Nevertheless, Colonel Matt Winn, Churchill Downs chairman, fined Ellis $100 for improper behavior.

Jesse Conley on Colston placed third and was the last black jockey to ride in the Derby, which had been so dominated by black jockeys and trainers in its early years, notably Isaac Murphy, Willie Simms and Jimmy Winkfield.

Meridian was a fine horse with a long record of stakes wins, including the National Handicap and Frontier Stakes as a three-year-old and four more stakes at four and five. He was second in the Queens County Handicap and third in both the Brookdale Handicap and Yonkers Handicap at the age of six.

Carroll Shilling hustles the tiring Worth, who led all the way and held off the last efforts of Duval and Flamma, the only filly in the race.

After Friday night's heavy rainfall, turfman Major T.C. McDowell thought it best to scratch The Manager, who did not run well in the mud, which left the field wide open for Worth in the 38th running. The colt was bought as a yearling by C.T. Worthington for $425 and was then turned over to the Gallagher Brothers for breaking. They were so impressed with the colt that they purchased him.

Worth won his first two races, was runner-up in an allowance race and then enjoyed a streak of seven wins. By Kentucky's spring racing season, Worth attracted the attention of many horsemen, including Frank Taylor, trainer for H.C. Hallenbeck, the wealthy New Yorker who then paid $3,500 for him. Worth closed his two-year-old season by winning a $10,000 private sweepstakes. The brown colt by Knight of the Thistle was proclaimed the two-year-old champion of 1911 with earnings of $16,645. He won 10 out of 11 starts.

After a slow start, Worth took the lead in the 1912 Derby and maintained an easy advantage under restraint, according to instructions from trainer F.M. Taylor to jockey Shilling. Meanwhile, Duval, a Kentucky horse, was gradually wearing down the field. He came alongside Worth and the two battled it out—with Johnny Loftus on Flamma, the only filly, making his move at them too late. The pair out front continued to duel, although Shilling never used the whip he held at the ready. Duval's nose was at Worth's throatlatch when Worth stumbled. The crowd groaned, but Shilling held Worth together and they flashed under the wire as East beat West one more time.

Carroll Shilling topped the list of leading jockeys in 1912 but Worth's career was abbreviated. He died as a three-year-old.

Donerail ✦ *May 10, 1913*

Owner-trainer T.P. Hayes and jockey Roscoe Goose pose with pride in front of Donerail, the 91-to-1 long shot.

*D*onerail paid $184.90 for a $2.00 win ticket in 1913—the longest odds and biggest payoff at the time. Owner Tom Hayes had decided to run the bay colt "just for the hell of it." It is one of the charms of racing that anything can happen, that anyone can win, as in 1973 when black trainer Harrison Johnson stunned Saratoga by winning the rich Hopeful Stakes with Gusty O'Shay, once claimed at Charlestown racetrack for $5,000.

Past the stands the first time in the thirty-ninth Derby, the favorite, Ten Point, was in the lead with Foundation two lengths back. Few noticed that Donerail was in the race. It was a two-horse contest up to the half-mile when the little Louisville boy, Roscoe Goose, who had been coasting in sixth on Donerail, realized he was shortening the distance to the front. His mount was running smoothly and by the stretch he was up with the leaders. Challenging and meeting every challenge, Donerail got his head and neck in front, and by the wire half of his body showed clear.

Donerail won for Hayes and made him the second and last man ever to breed, train and own a Derby winner. Not only that, Donerail set a new track record for the one-and-a-quarter miles, covering the distance in 2:14⁴/₅. The horse had done nothing better than third in two prior stakes. Roscoe Goose, however, had won 85 races that year and he set a record in death as in life. At the age of 81 he left an estate of $1.1 million—the wealthiest jockey of his era.

Goose began his great career inauspiciously, driving a delivery wagon, and ended it as a trainer who, among many successes to his credit, gave Charles Kurtsinger his first ride. Kurtsinger went on to win the roses twice—first with Twenty Grand in 1931 and then with War Admiral in 1937.

Old Rosebud ✦ May 9, 1914

Old Rosebud with Johnny McCabe up in a montage with John Madden, who bred not only Old Rosebud but the first Triple crown winner, Sir Barton (1919 Derby). All were foaled in the same red and black trimmed barn at his Hamburg Place near Lexington.

Old Rosebud was the first of five Derby winners bred by John Madden: Sir Barton (1919), Paul Jones (1920), Zen (1923) and Flying Ebony (1925). Madden, however, had let Old Rosebud go as a yearling for $500. (He owned only one winner in the Derby—Plaudit, in 1898.) So successful was Old Rosebud's first season that H.C. "Ham" Applegate turned down an offer of $30,000 for the bay gelding. As a two-year-old, Old Rosebud started 14 times, was second in two races and won the rest, making him the two-year-old champion of that season.

Since rain had not let up all night before Derby Day 1914, at dawn track superintendent Tom Young ordered his men to buy all the sponges available in Louisville and mop up the track by hand. With this feat accomplished, the track was so fast that Old Rosebud set a record of 2:03$^{2/5}$ that would stand until 1931.

"Hurry back, Johnny," called a stable boy to McCabe as he left the Downs paddock on the favorite. Old Rosebud burst to the lead and cut to the inside rail with Hodge hot on his heels. At the top of the stretch, Old Rosebud led Hodge who led the others. Bronzewing, the only filly in the race, was running "like a wild horse," picking up horses at the rear, and she was making for Hodge when the race ended. McCabe had opened Old Rosebud up to an eight-length lead at the wire and smashed Donerail's record of 1913 by 1$^{2/5}$ seconds.

Old Rosebud, plagued by lameness, went on to race more seasons than any other thoroughbred on record except for Exterminator (1918 Derby winner). Unraced at four and five due to a bowed tendon, he resurfaced at six and won 26 of his last 63 starts. He ran a total of 80 races and won 40. Old Rosebud fell victim to the fate of most geldings then: Having no future earning power as stallions, they were raced as long as possible. Still running at the age of 11, Old Rosebud snapped a foreleg going to the front and had to be destroyed.

Regret ✦ May 8, 1915

The lovely chestnut filly Regret with Joe Notter on board in front of the twin spires of Churchill Downs.

On May 8, 1915, Harry Payne Whitney's Regret became the first filly ever to win the Kentucky Derby. Regret was a star from the beginning of her career. As a two-year-old, she had won the Saratoga Special, the Sanford Memorial Handicap and the Hopeful Stakes at Saratoga—the only races she had ever entered and all were against colts. The Kentucky Derby was the first race of the great filly's third season. Despite a family loss when his brother-in-law drowned on the Lusitania the day before the Derby, H.P. Whitney, who had started 18 horses in the Derby (more than any other owner), started Regret.

Whitney feared that Regret might become skittish among the 15 colts, (the largest Derby field to date) and bolt on the first turn. But jockey Joe Notter, working on his season's winning percentage of .38, put her on the lead and in the clear immediately.

The daughter of Broomstick and granddaughter of Ben Brush, Regret took the lead at the start and never relinquished it. At the last eighth, she drew away from the nearest contender and won by two lengths easing up. Harry Payne Whitney said, "She has won the greatest race in America and I am satisfied."

Regret competed through her fifth year when she won the Gazelle Handicap and came second in the Brooklyn Handicap. Nineteen years after she had won the Derby, Regret died without producing a foal worthy of its mother.

The years of Donerail, Old Rosebud and Regret marked a significant turning point in the history of the Derby. Donerail had won at such astounding odds and set a track record. Old Rosebud had shattered that record the following year, and Regret had trounced 15 males and became the first filly to win. No longer could the Eastern racing establishment ignore their Southern peers. Churchill Downs had become the center of the Southern track establishment and the Derby was in truth the greatest race in the country again.

George Smith ✦ May 13, 1916

Johnny Loftus gives George Smith a morning "blowout" past a 16th pole at Churchill Downs prior to his Derby win. Portraits of jockey Johnny Loftus and owner John Sanford (inset).

One of the headlines the day after the 42nd Derby read "Whitney Out of Money," referring to Harry Payne's lack of luck with either Thunderer or Dominant, with whom he had wanted to repeat his win of the year before.

The Churchill Downs flower gardens were at their best, ablaze with red geraniums. Twelve three-year-olds had been entered for the 1916 contest and nine went to the post. Harry Payne Whitney's entry of Dominant and Thunderer were favored and Thunderer was undefeated. George Smith, John Sanford's black colt, had drawn the number eight post position.

George Smith was cleverly saved for the first three-quarters of a mile then went to the front, where he seemed to be safe until Star Hawk, making up incredible distances from way behind the pack, challenged him in the stretch. Supporters of both horses screamed themselves hoarse. Whipped and spurred unmercifully, Star Hawk chased the leader down the stretch and, like a hound about to make the kill, was alongside his shoulder when they passed under the wire. George Smith won like a frightened deer.

A montage of Matt Winn, track president, and Pancho Villa with winner Omar Khayyam and jockey Charles Borel in the winner's circle where it was then located in front of the grandstand.

Omar Khayyam was one of three Derby winners not born in this country (along with Tomy Lee and Northern Dancer). Foaled in England, the chestnut colt was purchased at Newmarket by the partnership of Billings and Johnson and sent to this country as a yearling. No one suspected he would win the Kentucky Derby at odds of 12 to 1. As a two-year-old, he had only one win to his credit and had been unplaced in his only start as a three-year-old prior to the Derby. After his win on May 12, Omar Khayyam had seven more straight wins and became the three-year-old champion and leading money winner for 1917 with earnings of $49,070.

Off to a slow start, Omar Khayyam gradually gained on the leaders and, saving ground on the far turn, was in contention with Ticket, who he outstayed at the finish, besting 14 other entries in another well-filled Derby. Midway closed a long distance to take third place. Omar Khayyam collected $16,600 in this single effort and continued to run through his fifth year. He retired to stud with a career total of $58,436.

Colonel Matt J. Winn not only ran Churchill Downs but several other racetracks throughout the country during his career. His travels often brought him into contact with widely known figures, including the notorious Mexican chieftain, Pancho Villa. Villa had a fancy for racing and assembled his string in the best way he knew how—by force. Winn had warned Ben Jones that Villa's men would be shopping at his barn and Jones had a groom heavily bandage one hindleg of his best horse, Lemon Joe. When Villa's henchmen saw the apparently broken-down animal, they took a horse that bore a resemblance to Jones' favorite instead.

Exterminator (left) with Willy Knapp works out with stablemate, Sun Briar, who had been first choice to run in the Derby.

The hottest contender for the 1918 Derby was W.S. Kilmer's Sun Briar. Exterminator had been purchased 10 days prior to the classic as a workhorse for Sun Briar, and when the favorite failed to train well, Exterminator went to the post in his stablemate's place and won in the mud at 30 to 1. As a two-year-old, Exterminator had started four times and won two unimportant races. The Derby was his first start at three years.

On the second Saturday in May Exterminator won easily. He moved up fast after the three-quarter mark and, slipping through on the rail, took the lead from Escoba who finished second. War Cloud, the favorite, met with interference on both turns and came in fourth behind Viva America. Thirty thousand people, most of them in shock and disbelief, and some of whom didn't know Exterminator was in the race, nonetheless cheered the courageous performance as the darkest of dark horses gave the best three-year-olds in the country a smart licking. It is not known if J. Cal Milam, the man who had sold Exterminator ten days before, was cheering.

In his long and distinguished career, the public grew to adore Exterminator and gave him names like "Old Bones," "Old Slim" and "Old Hatrack." Exterminator won at all distances, often under crushing weights, and was at his zenith at seven when he won 10 out of 17 starts carrying 132 pounds in all but two races. The public continued to make him the favorite long after his prime had passed. Having started in 100 races and won 50, he was a folk hero who retired when he was nine years old with an earnings record of $252,996.

Sir Barton · May 10, 1919

H.G. (for "Hard Guy") Bedwell, trainer, holds Sir Barton in the winner's circle with grim determination. Johnny Loftus scowls from the saddle.

It was another plum in the pocket of Kentucky's greatest all-round horseman, breeder and trainer, John Madden, affectionately called "The Wizard." Bred by Madden in partnership with Vivian Gooch of England, J.K.L. Ross' Sir Barton triumphed in this 45th running with ease and followed this victory by winning the Preakness and the Belmont Stakes, that trio of long-distance classics that columnist Charlie Hatton would later dub the "Triple Crown."

As the race began, Sir Barton broke well and took command with Eternal, considered his only threat, running second and Billy Kelly third. Sir Barton led until the final eighth where Loftus "shook him up" with his whip. Eternal faded into obscurity and Sir Barton triumphed five lengths to the good of Billy Kelly. When the chestnut colt crossed the Derby finish he was carrying 2½ pounds of overweight, some of which was assumed to be cocaine as Sir Barton was celebrated as one of the "great hopheads" of racing history. It was common in those days to "help a horse along." Ethics only forbade that a trainer run a horse "hot" one day and "cool" the next, thereby duping the bettors and sweetening their own purses. Many an old-timer reflects upon the pleasure of seeing his favorite parade in the paddock "with all his lights turned on."

Johnny Loftus piloted Sir Barton for his Triple Crown wins in 1919 and the great team were the best horse and rider of the year and the leading money winners. At Kenilworth Park in 1920 they lost a match race to Man o' War by seven lengths. It was "Big Red's" last race and a fitting way for him to retire, vindicating his only career loss the year before when Loftus had ridden him to a defeat by Upset and was held responsible.

Paul Jones ✦ May 8, 1920

An attendant steadies Paul Jones in the winner's circle of the 46th Kentucky Derby with jockey Ted Rice.

*D*ue to a press breakdown, the programs didn't arrive until just before the first race and the poor lad delivering them was mobbed, his jacket ripped and hat trampled by the zealous record crowd.

The 1920 Derby is best remembered as the Derby that Man o' War did not run in. His owner, Sam Riddle, thought the mandatory weight of 126 pounds, imposed this year for the first time, was too heavy and too soon in a three-year-old's career, especially over a long distance. He wisely spared "Big Red," called by his faithful groom, Will Harburt, the "mostest hoss," and eventually retired him in 1920 as America's greatest racehorse. So popular was he in Lexington that school children were directed to strew flowers in his path as he ambled into retirement, an order remanded by Riddle, saying he was, after all, "just a horse."

Clyde van Dusen proved his sire probably could have handled the distance when he won the Derby in 1929. And another son, War Admiral, took the Triple Crown in 1937 under the 126-pound weight.

Paul Jones, the long-shot winner, was almost beaten by the only horse ever to outrun Man o' War—Upset—who looked the winner at the 16th pole but tired at the wire. Paul Jones was sixth of seven geldings to win the Derby and the first gelding to win at level weights against colts. He ended his career after his fifth season with 14 wins in 65 starts.

Behave Yourself • May 7, 1921

Jockey Charles Thompson stands with Behave Yourself in his stall while H.J. "Derby Dick" Thompson and Colonel E.R. Bradley, the owner/trainer team responsible for three more Derby wins, plot further strategy.

It was the opening of the Spring Meeting at the Downs and the unofficial opening of straw-hat season, with the Fifth Avenue Dobbs straw the most "correct." The four hotels in town were full past capacity. People slept in the halls and stood in lines to dine at restaurants. The inconveniences were a small price to pay for Derbytime in the spring. Colonel Edward R. Bradley, a stone-faced gambler with a penchant for picking names for his horses beginning with the letter B, walked away from the 1921 Derby with close to $50,000 in prize money from his entries of Behave Yourself and Black Servant, who finished one and two. Harry Payne Whitney, whose entries of Prudery and Tryster had finished three and four, lost the $20,000 he so confidently dropped on their noses at the betting window.

Bradley had put the more successful jockey, Lyke, on Black Servant, and the less-known Thompson on Behave Yourself. Thompson had done well on the less prestigious "Far West" circuit, notably in Juarez, and Bradley had just purchased his contract, never expecting him to outdo himself so completely on May 7. Behave Yourself's career was also undistinguished before and after the Derby, but for that short period both horse and rider were at their prime. Behave Yourself was the first to go out to the post and the first to come home.

Colonel Bradley was reported to have been disappointed with the outcome of the Derby, as he had bet heavily on Black Servant. Behave Yourself had come second to Black Servant in the Blue Grass, a prep for the Derby. Bradley did, however, set two records, being the first to have owned and bred the one-two finishers in a Derby.

95

Morvich ✦ May 13, 1922

**Over an undulating field of straw hats, towers little Albert Johnson
aboard Morvich, the 1922 winner.**

Morvich, the black colt who had won 11 of his 11 starts as a two-year-old, was a favorite with the crowd of 75,000.

As the race started, a cry went up from the multitude in the stands and spread to the infield where thousands churned like a whirlpool turning to follow their horse. Morvich tore into the lead and running through the deafening corridor passed the stands with a one-and-a-half-length lead on Bradley's Busy American, the second favorite. But Busy American bobbled on the Clubhouse turn and was pulled up. My Play, a full brother to Man o' War, made a valiant reach for Morvich in the backstretch but was unsuccessful. Bet Mosie, who had lost a lot of ground going wide at both turns, made a tremendous effort at the last, closing the distance to lose by only a head to Morvich. Startle, the only filly in the race, lasted gamely for a mile, then faded.

When someone in the stands shouted that Morvich was done on the far turn, it caused a near hysteria and a soldier fell into the governor's box. Owner Benjamin Block teetered on a chair as his horse came in and was escorted by a jubilant throng to the winner's circle.

Morvich never won another race after the Derby, the effort under so much weight being too great for many Derby winners, but Colonel E.R. Bradley must have liked Albert Johnson's performance. He put him on Bubbling Over for the Derby of 1926, which they won.

Max Hirsh, the great trainer who would later run Derby winners Bold Venture (1936), Assault (1946) and Middleground (1950), may have regretted selling this colt he had purchased for a mere $4,000.

Zev ✦ May 19, 1923

Earl Sande on Zev goes immediately to the front in the 49th Kentucky Derby.

A week prior to the Derby, Zev finished 12th in the Preakness. Owner Harry F. Sinclair, whose involvement in the Teapot Dome Scandal would later be revealed, and trainer Sam Hildreth didn't bother to show up for the Derby. Only two people seemed loyal to Zev: his jockey, leading rider Earl Sande, and a boy from Paris, Kentucky, who had dreamed that Zev won the Derby and came with his life's savings of $200 and put it on the brown colt's nose. With his $3,800 winnings he announced that he would buy the family a home and take a long trip—all the way to Cincinnati.

Twenty-one of America's best three-year-olds came up to the starting web that year, the largest field in the race's history, among them the mud-running sprinter Zev, thought so out of place by the press. Sande, who had argued with owner and trainer to let the horse run, used Zev's quick speed to put him on top instantly and keep him there. Smooth and effortless, Zev ate up the track and opened up a two-and-a-half-length lead. Still running easily, he breezed around the oval with the rest of the field strung out behind him. Martingale, driving hard in second place, tried vainly to catch him but could never get closer than the one-and-a-half lengths he trailed by at the finish. Zev came in at odds of 19 to 1.

The handsome big black colt was sired by The Finn. His dam was Miss Kearney. Earl Sande would soon triumph with another son of The Finn in 1925—Flying Ebony. The $272,008 won by Zev in 1923, including the Derby, made him the year's leading money winner. Additionally, it was the most ever won in one year by an American racehorse.

Black Gold steps out onto the track with John Mooney for the Kentucky Derby's 50th Anniversary.

In 1909 Useeit, a pony-sized mare, raced against the larger, more experienced Belle Thompson at a dusty fairgrounds in Oklahoma. Although Useeit lost, she impressed Al Hoots, an Indian-Irish small-time rancher from Tulsa, who traded 80 acres of cattle grazing land for her. From the time of her purchase until 1916 the plucky mare raced 122 times, running in the money in 82 of those starts.

Her career ended abruptly on February 22, 1919, when she was claimed in a race in Mexico. Hoots refused to honor the claim, as there had been a gentlemen's agreement among the other owners not to claim Useeit, his love for the mare being common knowledge. Hoots chased off the waiting groom with a shotgun, packed the mare on a freight train to Oklahoma and was instantly barred from racing. As Hoots lay dying the following year he made his Osage Indian wife, Rosa, promise she would keep Useeit, breed her to Black Toney, Ed Bradley's great stallion, and run the result in the Kentucky Derby. Useeit was bred at Bradley's Idle Hour Farm in Lexington and a dark foal was born on February 17, 1921. He was named Black Gold for the oil that oozed in abundance out of the Oklahoma soil.

In spite of mismanagement and bad training on the part of Hedley Webb, who often ran Black Gold when he was dead lame, the colt won half his starts as a two-year-old and went off the favorite in the 50th "Run for the Roses"—the phrase invented that year by Bill Corum, who would take over track management in 1949. Black Gold came down the stretch with Chilhowee, Beau Butler and Altawood, all four within a head's distance of each other. Black Gold pulled away by a half-length at the wire and made Rosa Hoots the second woman in history to run a Derby winner.

Sporadically lame, Black Gold was raced through his fourth season and retired to stud where he proved to be sterile and so was returned to racing. In January 1928, the valiant Kentucky Derby winner broke a leg at the New Orleans Fair Grounds and was destroyed. A career that started at one fairground and ascended to the supreme pinnacle of American racing, ended at another where he lies today.

Flying Ebony ✦ *May 16, 1925*

A portrait of the powerful 51st Derby winner. The massive chest, sloping shoulder and dropped rump, much like Secretariat's, made for his success. (Inset) The young Earl Sande.

*I*n 1925 the Derby was a media event. Serious young men had wheeled in all kinds of technical equipment and had strung miles of wiring up to the top of the stands. "Credo" Harris, the director of WHAS Radio in Louisville, would announce the first broadcast of the Kentucky Derby. Over 6 million listeners worldwide were expected to tune in. The Derby was rapidly becoming a national sporting and social event, a triumph of the business and promotional talents of President Matt Winn who said, "My first love is the Kentucky Derby, and I've seen to it that the owners of three-year-olds with box office appeal flirt with no other stake but the Derby when Derbytime comes around."

Bill Corum's phrase, "Run for the Roses," had been picked up by newspapers and stations everywhere. This year's Derby resembled that of 1923. Although Earl Sande had persuaded Harry Sinclair to run Zev and won with him then, he could not get a ride for 1925. Turfwriters intervened, asking Gifford A. Cochran to start his Flying Ebony that Sande might ride. He acquiesced as a token of goodwill. Like Zev, Flying Ebony had been sired by The Finn at Madden's Hamburg Place.

As the horses paraded to the post, the heavens opened up and turned the track into a sea of mud—just the stuff Flying Ebony liked best. The rain stopped as fast as it had started but not before ruining the chances of the favorite, Quatrain, who despised the slop and finished up the track. Sande took Flying Ebony to the front just as he had done with his brother in 1923, leading all the way around against the field of over 20 horses. Captain Hal pushed his nose in front twice but gave in to Flying Ebony in the stretch. It was the first time a horse from the pari-mutuel field had won. Had he not been included in the field, his odds would have been impressive.

Bubbling Over, second from the right with the shadow-roll nose band he always wore, goes to the front at the start of the 52nd Kentucky Derby.

Kentuckian E.R. Bradley had a thing about the letter B, starting with a horse he named Bad News who traveled very fast. His busy Bs had a red letter year in 1926 with Bagenbaggage, Boot to Boot and Bubbling Over.

Bubbling Over was 7 for 10 and always in the money during his freshman campaign. However, the freshman championship laurels had gone to Pompey—considered to be Bubbling Over's main rival. Yet in the 52nd running, Bubbling Over had no real competition. Albert Johnson got him out in front immediately, set a torrid pace and galloped home the winner by five lengths. Bubbling Over's stablemate, Bagenbaggage, got a slow start but was running quickly at the end for the place money. It was the second time Colonel Bradley had sent out both the winner and the runner-up, having done so in 1921 with Behave Yourself and Black Servant. It was also a double for jockey Albert Johnson, who won with Morvich in 1922.

New York Mayor Jimmy Walker was there to present the trophy to the winner. Later he said, "I thought being elected mayor was the greatest thrill, but shucks, this is the thrill."

Bubbling Over broke down after the Derby and never raced again. But he was to make his presence felt in the Derby again when his son Burgoo King won in 1932.

"Ed" Bradley and his trainer, "Derby Dick" Thompson, dominated the Derby from his first entry in 1920 until his last in 1945. He often had as many as three horses in the classic, and if you didn't know what to bet, you "Bet Bradley." Bubbling Over, Burgoo King and Brokers Tip (1933) all came home first for Bradley's Idle Hour Farm.

Bradley was a gentleman gambler who backed down for no man, armed or not. In 1898 he opened his fabulous Palm Beach Club. Its popularity was attributed to the personality of its owner who never drank, swore or smoked.

Whiskery ✦ May 14, 1927

Harry Payne Whitney and James R. Keene, each of whom topped the country's list of leading owners many times, in front of Linus McAtee on Whiskery in Whitney's pale blue and coffee-brown silks.

Under a sky that alternately cleared and rained, the colorfully crowded stands seemed to glow and dim like houselights. The barrier flew up and the race was off to a fast start. "Chick" Lang on Jock literally flew to the lead and by the half-mile was five lengths in front. Meanwhile, Whiskery was deep in the pack but moved up to third position at the three-quarter pole. Osmand was running second as the three leaders hit the top of the stretch. Jock tired, leaving Whiskery and Osmand with Earl Sande driving hard to duel to the wire, where Whiskery prevailed by a blinkered head under a strong ride from "Pony" McAtee.

This was the second Derby win for Harry Payne Whitney, his talented filly Regret having triumphed in the 1915 running. The Whitney family would enter the Derby a total of 59 times and win twice more with Mrs. Payne Whitney's Twenty Grand in 1931 and Shut Out in 1942.

Had a quick-thinking groom not kept Whiskery's hind foot from wedging between his stall door and its frame as the horse rolled the morning of the race, there wouldn't have been a Whitney winner in 1929 and one that is so closely tied into Derby history. The 1896 winner, Ben Brush, was grandsire to both Meridian (1911) and Regret (1915), who were by Broomstick. Broomstick sired Whiskbroom II, who sired Whiskery. Prudery, Whiskery's dam, had run third in the Derby of 1921, and her sire, Peter Pan was the grand sire of Black Gold (1924). Whiskery was retired to stand at stud where he did not prove himself. He was returned to racing from which he was retired again and used as a field hunter until his natural death.

Reigh Count ✦ May 19, 1928

Reigh Count with "Chick" Lang up is led from the paddock where a field of straw hats envelopes the old Secretary's stand. (Inset) Owner, Mrs. John D. Hertz, the third woman after Mrs. C.E. Durnell and Rosa Hoots to own a Derby winner.

Reigh Count didn't win a race until his seventh start. When the colt finally did break his maiden, owner Willis Sharpe Kilmer was willing to let him go for "a pittance" to John D. Hertz, the Austrian immigrant who parlayed a few used cars into the Yellow Cab Company and later Hertz Rent-a-Car. Hertz had seen Reigh Count bite or "savage" another horse at the wire. It made a lasting impression on the former pugilist. The decision was made to run the horse under Mrs. Hertz's name.

Trainer Barney Michell quickly brought the "sulky" colt to hand for several important wins as a two-year-old. He then took an unusual route to the Derby, bringing Reigh Count up to the race on workouts alone. There, 21 rivals came to face the colt in the largest Derby to date. The crowd made Reigh Count the clear favorite. Jockey "Chick" Lang rated him patiently behind the leaders, picked up horses through the backstretch and got a head in front at the turn for home. At the wire Reigh Count was three lengths ahead of Misstep with speed in reserve.

Reigh Count went on to win many important stakes as a three-year-old. However, he did become a victim of the "graveyard of favorites" when he came up last in the Travers at Saratoga that August. He campaigned in England at four, winning the Coronation Cup and gaining a place in the Ascot Gold Cup. He was a most successful sire for the Hertzes, but his offspring included no Derby winners until Hertz bucked conventional wisdom and bred Reigh Count to an overraced, undistinguished mare named Quickly. The resulting ugly duckling of a foal was named Count Fleet, eventual winner of the Triple Crown (1943), who sired Count Turf, winner of the 1951 Derby.

Clyde Van Dusen • *May 18, 1929*

Clyde Van Dusen holds off Naishapur in the stretch run of the 55th Kentucky Derby.

The radio broadcasts that had begun just four years before had branched into a worldwide network bringing the Derby into homes everywhere. Despite the Wall Street crash, Derby enthusiasts will remember 1929 as the year that Jockey Linus "Pony" McAtee came back to Churchill Downs to repeat his victory of two years before on Whiskery. Only this time he rode a much smaller horse, an unusually high-spirited gelding named after his trainer, Clyde Van Dusen.

The day that jockey McAtee arrived to meet his Derby mount, trainer Van Dusen met him at the jockey's quarters to prepare him for his first glimpse of the horse. He tactfully explained to the jockey that although Clyde Van Dusen was very small he was fast and if McAtee could give him a good ride he could win. In spite of the preparation, McAtee's mouth dropped when he saw the size of the gelded son of Man o' War.

The low odds were on Colonel E.R. Bradley's entry of Blue Larkspur and Bay Beauty, who headed a field of 21 outstanding thoroughbreds. Just at post time the heavens opened up making the track a river of mud. With a rainfall of 1.17 inches that day the 55th Derby became one of the wettest on record. Clyde Van Dusen (the horse) had drawn post position number 20 and at the bell took off like a rocket. He was leading by the first quarter and saved ground while setting the pace. Naishapur, slow to start and racing wide, began moving up after going five-eighths, was blocked in the stretch, but came up again from 12th place past Panchio, who was running 2nd. At the finish it was Clyde Van Dusen by two lengths, Naishapur second by three and Panchio third. Blue Larkspur, the favorite, who had been shod for a dry track, finished fourth. Clyde Van Dusen had won $53,950 for his owner. After Clyde Van Dusen's successful four-year racing career, he was retired as a pensioner, a kindness now extended to geldings.

Gallant Fox ✦ May 17, 1930

A montage of trainer James "Sunny Jim" Fitzsimmons with Earl Sande on Gallant Fox and owner William Woodward of Belair Stud resting against President Roosevelt's limousine at Saratoga.

The great "Earl of Sande" had suffered severe leg injuries in a fall at Saratoga following his second Derby win on Flying Ebony in 1925 and had retired to train. William Woodward was determined to have Sande on his Gallant Fox and coaxed him out of retirement.

Gallant Fox, an impressive bay colt by Sir Gallahad III, was the crowd favorite of the 15 three-year-olds from the best stables in the country. Both Fitzsimmons and Sande had expressed their confidence in the colt. According to the odds makers, the only horse Gallant Fox had to beat was E.F. Prichard's Tannery.

A persistent drizzle did not alter the condition of the track. The horses were led into the stalls of the first mechanical gate used at the Downs and, when the bell clanged, got off to a perfect start. Gallant Fox was in tight quarters for the first three-eighths of a mile, then he broke loose from the pack and swung wide to the outside. Passing horse after horse, he took over the lead in the backstretch. From then on the race belonged to him. At the finish, he led by two lengths to the good of Gallant Knight, who had made a strong bid at the mile but couldn't keep pace with "that handy guy named Sande bootin' a winner in." Tannery, a victim of the blistering pace, finished "up the track."

Gallant Fox won the Preakness and the Belmont Stakes to become the second Triple Crown winner, after Sir Barton in 1919. His Derby win initiated a 10-year dominance of the Derby by Woodward, Fitzsimmons and Belair. The "Fox of Belair" would be the only Triple Crown winner to sire a Triple Crown winner, Omaha, whose triple wins came in 1935. Another offspring, Johnstown, would come close with a 10-length win in the 1939 Derby and triumph in the Belmont Stakes. In this third Derby win, Sande tied Isaac Murphy's win record but outdistanced him by going on to take the Triple Crown. Sande's record would stand until 1938 when the master of the craft, Eddie Arcaro, would start his Derby blitz of five wins with Lawrin in 1938.

Twenty Grand at the head of the pack on the far turn in Mrs. Whitney's watermelon pink and black silks barely misses hitting spectators who pile on top of each other on the infield rail.

Tens of thousands of Derby fans had arrived for the 57th running, and Bowman Field was packed with private "two-seaters" and the giant 30-passenger Fokker transports. By noon the grandstand was filled beyond capacity with dapper gentlemen and lovely women in silk shantung, chiffons and polka dots that blended in a shifting cataract of color.

The track was lightning fast. Not only did Twenty Grand whip through the mile-and-a-quarter distance in a record time of 2:01⁴/₅, but Gallant Knight, second in the Derby the year before, had thrilled the crowd in the race just before this Derby by setting a world record for six-and-a-half furlongs in 1:16²/₅.

An even dozen of the nation's best three-year-olds paraded to the mechanical gate without the wonderful Equipoise (scratched due to an injury), who had pushed Twenty Grand to a record for the mile the year before in a nose-to-nose duel. Twenty Grand started slowly. Taking him to the outside, Kurtsinger gradually brought him past the pack after the half-mile and wore down Sweep All at the front. With a tremendous show of energy he widened the gap to four lengths and passed under the wire with speed to spare.

It was the first of two Derby wins for Kurtsinger who would triumph again on War Admiral in 1937. Twenty Grand won the Wood Memorial, Belmont Stakes, Travers and Jockey Club Gold Cup that year, and was then retired to stud where he did not distinguish himself. He was returned to racing in his seventh year but without much success.

Eugene James headed for the post on Burgoo King, in E.R. Bradley's green and white silks, past the crowded extension of the grandstand. (Inset) Colonel Bradley and "Derby Dick" Thompson.

The Depression was showing some effect on the Derby by 1932, at least in the wagering, which this year would be less than half of the three years before. The favorite for the 58th Run for the Roses was Loma Stable's great colt, Tick On, over the Bradley entry of Burgoo King and Brother Joe. Burgoo King, an impressive colt by Bubbling Over, Bradley's 1926 winner, was named for James T. Looney, who popularized the local stew across the nation and was dubbed the "Burgoo King." Although Burgoo King had not won a stakes race in his two-year-old career, Bradley was willing to bet anyone $5,000 that he could beat their horse the first time they met as three-year-olds. There were no takers.

Just prior to the start, 5,000 fans broke through the back side fence and poured into the infield as the police stood by helpless. For 15½ minutes the field of 20 waited at the start with Tick On creating most of the disturbance. Finally off, Economic took the lead and dominated the race until the top of the stretch. Burgoo King, possibly feeling the effects of his cod liver oil and fish liver diet, fairly leaped from the pack and with a tremendous stretch drive passed Economic and pulled away to a five-length win.

The 19-year-old Eugene James from Louisville spoke proudly of his win into the Movietone microphone with the same direct forthrightness that carried Burgoo King down the stretch for Bradley's second Derby triumph. Burgoo King would go on to win the Preakness and retire to produce many stakes winners until his death in 1946 at the age of 17.

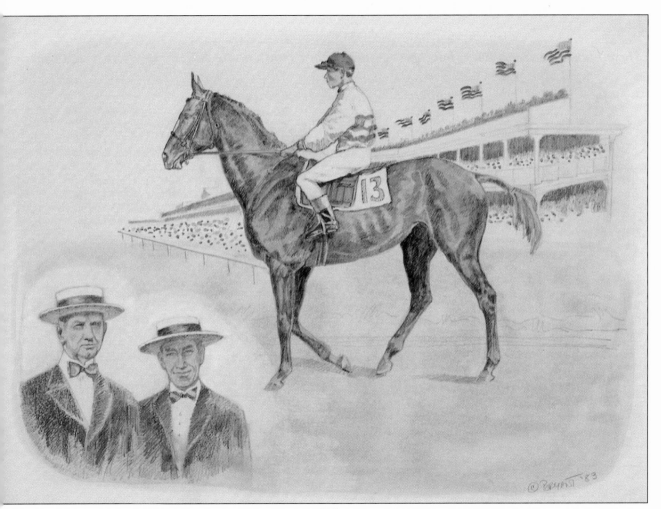

Brokers Tip ✦ May 6, 1933

Herb Fisher on Head Play (left) grabs for Brokers Tip's saddlecloth as he drives past him on the inside rail. Jockey Don Meade tries to push Fisher away in the homestretch of the "Rodeo Derby."

E.R. Bradley, the first man to breed and own three Derby winners, never expected to do it a fourth time with Brokers Tip, who never won another race. Brokers Tip, the son of Black Toney, sire of Black Gold (1924) was born with a half-deformed foot and couldn't stand on his own as a weanling. Shod with the weak foot raised on leather pads, Brokers Tip made it to the races at two but never won.

Head Play, bought by Willie Crump for $500, was sold to Mrs. Silas B. Mason the day before the Derby for $30,000 plus 15 percent of the purse if he won (and he was favored).

A light breeze groomed the track to perfection as the bugle called the 13 horses from the paddock. The field got off to a good start. Head Play went to the front while Brokers Tip stayed at the rear. At the top of the stretch, jockey Herb Fisher, unaware that Brokers Tip was coming up behind him, took Head Play wide to ride out Charley O, a fatal mistake as Don Meade then pushed Brokers Tip through the hole left by Head Play. Fisher, thinking he had the race won, came back in to battle neck and neck with Brokers Tip, but Head Play was "out of gas" from running wide, and Fisher made his desperate lunge to stop Meade. Past the wire, Fisher stood in his stirrups and slashed at Meade with his whip. As the official sign went up declaring Brokers Tip the winner, Fisher sat down and cried. Back in the jockey's room, he attacked Meade and they fought viciously until reporters and valets broke them up. Though "foul riding" was not uncommon, it was usually done with more discretion. Derby mania had simply carried Fisher away.

Cavalcade in front of one of the barns at Brookmeade trimmed in the blue and white colors of the "Mistress of Brookmeade," Mrs. Isabel Dodge Sloan (inset).

In 1934, Isabel Dodge Sloan, of the automobile industry fortune, was named leading owner—a first in racing history for a woman. Inheriting $7 million on the death of her father, John F. Dodge, Mrs. Sloan went a'-racing, first with steeplechasers and then on the flat. She purchased Cavalcade (who was conceived in England but born in this country) at Saratoga as a yearling for $1,200.

The Derby enjoyed a capacity crowd, welling to over capacity when gate-crashers rushed past the token police force. The next year the National Guard would be called in to maintain order and put an end to gate-crashing for all time. The media was out in force with both WHAS for CBS and WAVE for NBC covering the event along with a sea of popping flashbulbs and clicking shutters.

Thirteen horses burst from the gate and Mata Hari jumped to a lead she held at the mile. Cavalcade, who had broken slowly, was steadily creeping toward the front with Discovery hot on his heels. At the top of the stretch Discovery had captured the lead, with Cavalcade alongside. Cavalcade wore down Discovery and pulled away to a handsome victory. The usually dignified and sedate Mrs. Sloan screamed herself silly.

Jockey Willie Garner had tried 13 times to win the Derby and had come the closest with a second on Misstep in 1928. After 20 years of riding races, his horse led in the Derby homestretch. It was also a satisfying victory for trainer R.A. Smith, who had inadvertently muffed his first try at the racing game. As a lad in 1887, he'd paid $210 at Sheepshead Bay for a runt of a colt, so badly did he want a horse of his own. Ridiculed for the young horse's appearance, Smith sold the colt, who later became Tenny, Salvator's great match-race rival.

Omaha ✦ May 4, 1935

Omaha with Willie "Smokey" Saunders strides out onto the track at Churchill Downs under the red and white polka-dot silks of William Woodward's Belair Stud.

The 61st running of the Kentucky Derby would be photographed by the Standard Gravure Corporation for reproduction in the *Courier-Journal* newspaper. The time needed to reproduce the event for the public would be only one-and-three-quarter hours, not exactly instant replay but a remarkable achievement for the times. The Derby betting pool climbed back to its $1 million mark of four years before and the gate-crashers were trounced by the National Guard.

In spite of the rain and the unseasonably cold weather, the stands were packed. The favorite that day carried the new but soon-to-be-famous silks of Calumet Farm. The horse was Nellie Flag, the first filly favorite in the Derby, ridden by a jockey destined for immortality, Eddie Arcaro. Omaha, the chestnut son of Triple Crown winner Gallant Fox, was also favored along with E.R. Bradley's Boxthorn. Eighteen horses started from the so-called mechanical gate, in this case an arrangement of free-standing padded dividers with a wire strung from end-to-end in front that sprung upward at the bell. The Kentucky-born Omaha avoided the crowding that caught Nellie Flag and, running wide, took command at the half-mile and romped on home, much in the style of his dad five years before. "Smokie" Saunders said it was "a cinch" and passed out his roses. "He won in a romp," gushed his owner, the staid president of the New York Jockey Club, William Woodward. Then he hugged a reporter.

Gallant Fox never had the chance to show his full potential, but through his son, Omaha, ran and triumphed again over the same courses. With wins in the Preakness and the Belmont Stakes, Omaha made his sire the only Triple crown winner to sire a Triple Crown winner. Like so many great racehorses, however, Omaha was a failure at stud.

Bold Venture ✦ May 2, 1936

Brevity goes to his knees as Bold Venture starts well in the brown and white colors of M.L. Schwartz at the beginning of the Kentucky Derby.

The 62nd Run for the Roses was strewn with thorns. The favorite, Brevity, fell at the start. Eventual Horse of the Year, Granville, unseated his rider. World-record holder for the mile-and-an-eighth, Indian Broom, was badly blocked. Bold Venture was in close quarters, too, but jockey Ira "Babe" Hanford steered him out of trouble and into the lead. He Did lost all hope of a late rally when a long-armed spectator standing on the inner rail of the last turn reached out and grabbed jockey Charles Kurtsinger's whip. At the wire, it was Bold Venture holding a head advantage over the colt that many thought had run the best race—Brevity, who overcame his stumble at the start, was forced to race wide, yet covered a tremendous amount of ground to miss catching the winner by a head. After the race, three jockeys were barred from the track for 15 days for rough riding, including Ira Hanford.

Although trained by the esteemed Max Hirsch, Bold Venture appeared outclassed by the talented Derby field. He had never won a stakes and was being ridden by an apprentice jockey—no apprentice had ever won a Derby. Bold Venture was to prove, however, that his performance in the Derby was no fluke. A week later he took the Preakness, withstanding another furious stretch duel, this time with Granville, who had managed to keep his jockey in the saddle. Bold Venture bowed a tendon after the Preakness and was retired. But the horse was lucky enough to be alive. On a trip back from Saragota his railroad car had caught on fire. Groom Rufus "Do Right" Scott beat back the flames for mile after mile to save the colt's life.

War Admiral ✦ *May 8, 1937*

**War Admiral with Charles Kurtsinger walks up toward owner Sam Riddle
and trainer George Conway.**

*B*y 1937, the Derby had become so popular and overcrowded that spectators made cheap cardboard periscopes in an attempt to get some view of the proceedings. Most heard rather than saw War Admiral's classic performance.

War Admiral's sire, Man o' War, may have been the greatest racehorse ever. But War Admiral was to do something his father never did—win the Kentucky Derby. Sam Riddle, who owned and bred both, never cared for the Derby and had held Man o' War out of it. To him, Churchill Downs was an upstart track, and its long-distance classic came too early in the year for not quite mature three-year-olds.

On the small side like his mother and something of a late bloomer like his father, War Admiral finally got going at the end of his two-year-old season by winning three out of six starts and was never out of the money. He was the favorite in this Derby over 19 rivals—including the two-year-old champion, Pompoon—but War Admiral had a distinct aversion to the starting gate and held up the Derby start for eight-and-a-half minutes while his handlers tried to wedge him into his stall. Yet when the gates finally sprang open he was all business. He flew to the lead and stayed there to the wire, holding off Pompoon by almost three lengths.

"The Admiral's" Preakness win may have been the most exciting race of the year. He and Pompoon battled up to the stretch, neck and neck every step of the way except the last, where War Admiral got a nose in front. He then gave jockey Charles Kurtsinger, "the Flying Dutchman," a rocking-chair ride in his easy Belmont win to become American Racing's fourth Triple Crown champion.

Lawrin ✦ May 7, 1938

A portrait of the 1938 Derby winner.

The big winner on Derby Day was Herbert M. Woolf. Not only did he own Lawrin, but he backed him heavily at attractive odds, and cashed an estimated $150,000 in pari-mutuel tickets. Herbert Woolf had been a prominent breeder of saddle breds, but witnessing the Derby of 1929 convinced him to acquire a stable of racehorses. He campaigned the Kansas-bred Lawrin heavily, starting him 23 times before the Churchill Downs meet without impressive results. His jockey, Eddie Arcaro, weighed only three pounds when he was born in Cincinnati. Sickly as a child, he toughened up at local "bush league" tracks in Kentucky.

As the race got underway, Arcaro rated his mount through the early going, hugging the rail and saving every bit of precious ground. By the top of the stretch Lawrin had the lead by three lengths, but with an eighth-of-a-mile to go, his drive for the wire wilted and he started to drift into the center of the track. Dauber was gaining with every stride, but the race was over before he pulled even with the winner. The Derby win would remain the highlight of this Kansas shipper's career.

Mrs. Payne Whitney's contract with Arcaro allowed him to ride for other stables if Greentree was not entered, which is how Arcaro was free to ride Lawrin for trainer Ben Jones; Arcaro and Jones would collaborate on three more Derby wins.

Johnstown as a stud in later years with his trainer, James "Sunny Jim" Fitzsimmons, as an older man.

New backstretch bleachers were opened in 1939 and the 20,000 in attendance took advantage of the 50¢ admission and the $1 bets available there. A few dozen enterprising and fearless fans shimmied up two telephone poles across the street from the track and lashed a crossbar between them. From that vantage point they watched Johnstown show why he was the overwhelming favorite.

Johnstown, nicknamed the "Old Man of the Mountains," counted four stakes among his seven wins as a two-year-old. At age three he set the track record at Jamaica Park for a mile-and-seventy yards and equaled the course standard in the Wood. His odds were the shortest in 34 and the field of eight was the smallest of the last 21 Derbies.

Jockey James Stout got Johnstown out to the lead soon after the start and there he stayed uncontested. The big Kentucky bred put on a show in the stretch, drawing clear to an eight-length advantage. Nick Wall, who rode El Chico, said, "All I'm thankful for is that Stout didn't whack Johnstown across the rear end once during the whole race because if he had'a Johnstown would have won by a half-mile."

For Stout this impressive win was vindication for the 1936 Derby in which he was unseated by Granville at the post. Johnstown was the third Kentucky Derby winner for trainer "Sunny Jim" Fitzsimmons. And Johnstown's owner, William Woodward, in just ten years and with only six tries had run three Derby winners (Gallant Fox, 1930, and Omaha, 1935). Great though he thought Johnstown was, Woodward was not ready to concede that this colt was the equal of his favorite, Gallant Fox.

Gallahadion ✦ May 4, 1940

Gallahadion, in the orange, chocolate and white colors of Mrs. Ethel Mars of the Mars candy company, fights to outlast Bimelech in the stretch of the 66th Derby.

In 1940, a Bradley horse named Bimelech went off at even shorter odds than Johnstown had the year before. Bimelech was the shortest priced Derby horse since the advent of pari-mutuel wagering.

As "Derby Dick" Thompson, Bradley's first-string trainer, had died when Bimelech was two, the aging Bill Hurley took over his duties. Where the first could be criticized for training too hard, Hurley had a tendency to train too soft. Left in Kentucky to fatten over the winter, Bimelech was not put into hard work until early spring. The two-year-old champ won the Blue Grass easily but was strained after the race. Yet Hurley ran Bimelech two days later in the Derby trial, which he won, trouncing Gallahadion and other hopefuls. But the effort had ruined his Derby chances.

Gallahadion wore down his highly touted rival in the final furlong on Derby Day. The long-shot players in the crowd were rewarded with $74.20 for every $2.00 bet. Few had given this colt any chance to win, but trainer Roy Waldron had been predicting victory for his Gallahadion all week. Perhaps most surprised by the outcome was jockey Carroll Bierman. He had never been aboard Gallahadion and considered Bimelech to be the best horse in America. His riding strategy was simple—to save all the ground he could. He negotiated Gallahadion to a one-and-a-half-length win.

It was a sweet victory for owner Ethel V. Mars, who had parlayed her husband's candy bar fortune into a top racing stable known as the "Stars of the Milky Way." Illness forced her to follow the proceedings over the radio. Her daughter said, "I'm sure mother would have fainted had she not already been in bed."

Gallahadion ran a few more respectable races but would never again be a stakes winner.

Whirlaway ✦ *May 3, 1941*

Whirlaway, as a stallion at Calumet Farm where he was raised, strikes a handsome pose as owner Warren Wright proudly holds his lead shank. He was the first of eight Derby winners bred and run by Calumet and the first of their two Triple Crown champions.

The crowd of 100,000 for the 67th running poured almost $2 million into the pari-mutuel machines, the most wagered since 1926, and they were rewarded with a record-shattering performance. The paper the next day referred to Whirlaway's eight-length victory as a "blitzkrieg" and the battle for place "rear-guard action."

Whirlaway was bred for this Derby which his great-grandsire, Ben Brush, had won. As a two-year-old, "Whirly" never displayed the great stretch drive which would become his trademark. In the Blue Grass Stakes, a Derby prep race, he bore out. In the Derby Trial, he showed a startling burst of speed around the far turn but made a beeline for the outer rail. Trainer Ben A. Jones admitted that "Whirly" was the dumbest horse he'd ever trained. When asked if Whirlaway was a half-wit, Jones replied, "I don't know, but he's making a half-wit out of me." Jones corrected Whirly's problem: he cut a hole in Whirly's left blinker and got Eddie Arcaro to work the horse next to the inside rail

In the Derby, Whirlaway hung back early on but by the stretch he was clear by three lengths and made directly for the wire: he put eight lengths between his long flying tail and the rest. "Mr. Longtail" had taken 2/5 of a second off Twenty Grand's 1931 record and won both the Preakness and Belmont in the same blitzkrieg style to become the fifth horse to earn the Triple Crown. Said Arcaro, "[Riding Whirlaway] was like gunning a Cadillac. How he could pour it on!"

Shut Out ✦ *May 2, 1942*

Shut Out goes postward with Wayne Wright in the irons. Mrs. Payne Whitney (inset) became the first woman to own two Derby winners, her first being Twenty Grand in 1931.

The Derby crowd sported a new fashion look in 1942—uniforms. The soldiers, sailors and marines were reminders that most of the world was at war. In the betting shed both pari-mutuel tickets and war bonds were sold.

The crowd had picked the Greentree Stable entry as the favorite because of Devil Diver, not because of his lightly regarded stablemate, Shut Out. Sharing the crowd's appraisal was jockey Eddie Arcaro. Even after piloting Shut Out to an impressive Blue Grass Stakes score, the Kentucky Italian chose Devil Diver for the Derby and gave Shut Out to a scrappy Idaho rider named Wayne Wright who wanted to make a comeback. Shut Out started off smartly, pressing the pace, and then drew clear in the stretch by over two lengths. Arcaro and Devil Diver finished sixth. Arcaro chose Devil Diver again for the Preakness Stakes, and again they finished behind Shut Out, who did not win this classic. Shut Out returned for the Belmont, this time with Arcaro, who had seen the light, and they won. The pair went on to repeat the performance in the Travers at Saratoga.

Shut Out was the last son of the great Equipoise. Like Man o' War, Equipoise won just about everything there was to win in horse racing but the Kentucky Derby, which he had been favored to win until he came up lame just prior to Derby Day. Like Man o' War and War Admiral, winning the Derby was a task Equipoise left to his son.

137

Count Fleet ✦ May 1, 1943

Jockey Johnny Longden gives Count Fleet an early morning workout. Count Fleet made his owner, Mrs. John Hertz, the second woman in Derby history to run two winners (Reigh Count, 1928), after Mrs. H.P. Whitney's Twenty Grand in 1931 and her Shut Out the year before Count Fleet.

The 1943 Derby crowd came to Churchill Downs in streetcars because of wartime gasoline restrictions. Not one of John Hertz's yellow cabs was in evidence when Count Fleet won the 1943 Derby.

Reigh Count had sired many winners but until "The Count" no champions. Before giving up on the stallion completely, Hertz bred Reigh Count, a "stayer," to speed in the form of a swift mare named Quickly. The resulting ugly duckling became something of a rogue. Hertz tried to unload Count Fleet several times, but jockey Johnny Longden realized that the colt was a "runner" and prevailed upon Hertz not to sell him, whereupon Hertz prevailed upon Longden to do the riding.

The Count started well at two, but then lost a couple of important stakes, including the Futurity, at Belmont, where he clung to a filly named Askmenow. Said Longden, "For the last three-eighths he laid on Askmenow and I couldn't drag him off." But that was the last defeat of his career.

He and nine rivals made it to Churchill Downs where he got right out to the front, coasting to an easy three-length win. In the Preakness he stretched the winning margin to eight lengths, and for the Belmont he drew clear by an incredible 25. He had warmed up for the third leg of the Triple Crown by romping in the Withers as well. But winning the Triple Crown was to be Count Fleet's last accomplishment as a racehorse. He had injured himself in the Belmont and was never able to return to the track. Like his sire, Reigh Count, Count Fleet also sired a Derby winner—1951 champion, Count Turf. It was the first three-generation sweep of the event.

139

Pensive ✦ *May 6, 1944*

Pensive and Conn McCreary in the red and blue silks of Calumet Farm break from the gate.

The favorite May 6 was Greentree Stable's Stir Up with jockey Eddie Arcaro under contract to Greentree. Calumet's Pensive brought back memories of Cavalcade's 1934 Derby. Both were sired by and out of English horses. Cavalcade, by Lancegaye out of Hastily, had been imported to this country while still carried by Hastily. In 1940, England's Lord Astor sold a mare named Penicuik II to an American breeder on the condition that Penicuik II be bred to Hyperion, the English Derby winner. Penicuik II was purchased by Warren Wright shortly before she foaled the chestnut colt, Pensive, who would become the Kentucky Derby's 70th winner.

The condition of the track was good in spite of a 36-hour deluge, which had finally ended the afternoon before the race. Sixteen three-year-olds went to the post. Aboard Pensive, little Conn McCreary was looking for his first Derby win in four starts. The gates opened and Pensive was fourth in the early running. McCreary took Pensive back to 13th, but by the mile had moved him up to fifth on the inside. Hugging the rail, his chestnut coat gleaming, the big colt flew by the leaders as if they were standing still. At the finish Pensive was ahead of his nearest rival by four-and-a-half lengths. Stir Up and Arcaro finished third.

This was Calumet's second Derby win and the awesome winning machine that would take six more had begun to roll. It was trainer Ben A. Jones' third winner, putting him just one victory behind trainer "Derby Dick" Thompson of Idle Hour.

Hoop Jr. ✦ June 9, 1945

**Fred Hooper holds Hoop Jr. with Eddie Arcaro up. Trainer I.H. Parke
and friends pose in their flamboyant suits and hats in the style of the forties.**

*B*ecause of a wartime effort to curb unnecessary transportation, the Derby was run almost a month late. Over 80,000 spectators filled Churchill Downs. Eddie Arcaro would win his third Derby, equaling the records of Isaac Murphy and Earl Sande. Murphy had won his third in 1891, and Sande back from retirement, won his third on Gallant Fox in 1930.

Arcaro and Calumet's Ben Jones had scored two Derbies together, but in 1944 Jones pulled ahead when he assigned Conn McCreary to Pensive, who beat Arcaro and Stir Up. In this Derby, Arcaro evened the score with Hoop Jr. and beat the Ben Jones-trained Pot O'Luck. The team of Jones and Arcaro would win again in 1948 and 1952.

Pot O'Luck was the slight favorite over Hoop Jr., and the entire field was soaked to the skin. The track was lost in water. A healthy roar went up from the infield and the stands when the horses broke from the gate. Starting from the 12th "hole," Hoop Jr. was in charge by the first quarter, with Buymeabond keeping pace just behind. Pot O'Luck had moved up quickly to eighth and was driving hard. Running almost without effort in the stretch, Hoop Jr. opened the gap to six lengths over Pot O'Luck at the wire.

Hoop Jr. was the fist yearling purchase by Fred Hooper, the Florida contractor who said after the Derby win, "I never thought I'd make it so quick." Having won the Wood Memorial, the Kentucky Derby and placed second in the Preakness, Hoop Jr. was retired to stud service.

Assault ✦ May 4, 1946

In the paddock, jockey Warren Mehrtens, trainer Max Hirsch and Robert Kleberg of the King Ranch admire Assault before Mehrtens gets a "leg up."

O ver 105,000 war-weary Americans made their way to Churchill Downs for the first peacetime Kentucky Derby since Whirlaway's. A move to ban liquor from the race meeting was quashed. To women especially, the 1946 race will be remembered as the "Hat Derby." The Hedda Hopper variations caused women's heads to turn but annoyed serious horsemen whose views were blocked. One hat that could not go unnoticed was an extravaganza of apples, flowers and ivy in triple tiers; another featured turtles.

Robert Kleberg of the King Ranch in Texas, had bought the Max Hirsch-trained Bold Venture (Derby, 1936) from M.L. Schwartz for stud purposes and got Assault and Middleground from him. Both won the Derby under Hirsch's guidance. Assault became one of the top horses of the century, as he won the Preakness and Belmont, and thus became the seventh Triple Crown king in spite of his deformed foot. (Brokers Tip had won the Derby 1933 with a bad foot but did nothing else.)

The race that day was never even close. The "Club-footed Comet," as he was affectionately called, started from a good post position, stayed with the leaders for the first mile and, turning for the stretch, effortlessly skimmed through on the rail. He was two-and-a-half lengths in front at the one-sixteenth pole and, at the finish, he was eight lengths to the good of Spy Song with Hampden third.

Jet Pilot ✦ May 3, 1947

Jet Pilot enjoying his retirement.

I t was still the Big Band era. While the "chic" partied at the famous Galt House, Sealbach or Brown Hotel, others in "zoot suits" and fringes whooped it up to the beat of washboard bands. The parties continued for a week until the dawn of Derby Day.

The year before the 73rd running, a disastrous fire had destroyed most of Main Chance Farm's stable of two-year-olds valued at $282,000. Luckily, Jet Pilot had just been shipped to Churchill Downs with Mrs. Graham's Derby hopefuls for 1946. He won his first time out as a two-year-old at the Downs and three more times in 11 outings before returning to Churchill for the 1947 Derby.

The heavy favorite to win was C.V. Whitney's Phalanx. Also favored was Calumet's Faultless ridden by Eddie Arcaro, now back on the team with Ben Jones. Jet Pilot, sired by Blenheim II, Whirlaway's sire, took command of the race in much the same style as Whirlaway. Favored second on the boards he settled for nothing less than first. From start to finish Jet Pilot played "catch me" and nobody could but it was close. Under a strong hand-ride from Eric Guerin, he outlasted Phalanx with Faultless breathing down their necks. The judges had to consult the photograph before announcing the result. It was the first photo finish in Derby history.

Eddie Arcaro and Citation after their 1948 Derby victory.

*W*arren Wright had sold his Calumet baking powder company for $28 million one year before the crash of 1929 and put a large portion of it into horse racing. His wife, Lucille, had told Ben Jones when he was hired that winning the Derby was the most important thing in her life. Hiring as many as 60 employees at a time, Jones kept all his figures in his head and consulted frequently with his grooms and riders. As a result, they did not stray. The Calumet string was divided between Jones and his son Jimmy, and they cleaned up races on both coasts as well as the Midwest. Keeping up with the Jones boys was nearly impossible.

Not since the great Man o' War had the racing establishment had a champion of the caliber of Citation. Arcaro would say he was the best horse he ever rode, though Whirlaway was more exciting. Calm, cool and collected, Citation ran with a frictionless stride, often glancing at scenery when he was on the lead. With a fine head and intelligent eye he was so uncomplicated a "Chinaman could train him," according to Ben Jones. In February of 1948 Ben Jones had cut loose on the racing world another sensation—Coaltown, who many thought might best Citation and Arcaro in the Derby. Eddie had made the wrong choice before, riding Greentree's Devil Diver instead of Shut Out in 1942. When he asked Jones if he was on the right horse, Jones told him that if Coaltown could win he'd be on him. Calumet's entry of Citation and Coaltown in the 74th Derby was so awesome that only four other stables bothered to enter. Citation, the favorite, had opened in the winter book at odds of 8 to 5 that dropped to 4 to 5 before Derby Week. The other horses in the race were there in hopes that Citation and Coaltown would bump into each other and fall down.

Coaltown led in the mud up the backstretch. Arcaro clucked to "Cy" at the quarter pole and he breezed home three-and-a-half lengths ahead—with ears up. Citation won the Preakness and Belmont just as casually and 19 out of 20 races at age three for $865,000 in lifetime earnings. But Warren Wright wanted the $1 million mark and Cy complied, despite tendon trouble. Just one year after Wright's death, Citation became America's first equine millionaire.

Ponder ✦ May 7, 1949

Away slowly from the gate, Steve Brooks on Ponder artfully picks up horses on the backstretch in the inevitable devil's red and blue hoops of Calumet.

This was the Derby's Diamond Jubilee—or 75th year. Ponder would be the fourth of Calumet's eight Derby winners. With three seconds, one third, and two fourths in 17 starts, no other racing stable would come close. Colonel E.R. Bradley with half as many winners was the nearest contender.

Ponder was one of the few Calumet starters Ben Jones had little hopes for, saying that he would be content with a piece of the purse. But Ponder had won the Derby Trial against many of the same horses the Tuesday before, which should have been some indication of his capabilities. The son of Pensive (Derby, 1944), Ponder would surprise them all, as his sire had done, and run the course in exactly the same time (2:04⅕).

The outstanding favorite was Fred Hooper's Olympia with Eddie Arcaro in the saddle. Ben Jones had said nothing in the race could come close to Olympia, especially his "poor li'l ol' horse." Whether or not he was playing possum we'll never know, but Ponder won on May 7, paid $34 on a $2 bet and made fools of the experts.

As predicted, Olympia bolted to the front with Capot close behind. Palestinian had worked his way up to third. Ponder, off to a late start, was catching horses on the outside on his way to the leaders. At the far turn he was sixth and coming hard. Then in the stretch he weakened, fell back to fourth, but collected himself and came on again flying up to challenge Capot and Palestinian. As they came down to the wire, it was Ponder all alone and three lengths in front.

"Plain Ben" was one of the few people surprised to find himself back in the winner's circle. His unplanned win had set a trainer's Derby record—five wins in all—exceeding "Derby Dick" Thompson's score by one.

Middleground as he was at age three. Inset: Trainer Maximilian Justice Hirsch.

*C*olonel Matt J. Winn, architect of the Derby as we know it, died before this race. He had seen every Derby, from 1875 to 1949 and had served as its guiding force since 1902, when he and some investors bought the failing track. He was succeeded by Bill Corum.

Fifteen of the country's best three-year-olds stood in the gate with Your Host, Hill Prince, Oil Capitol, Middleground, Mr. Trouble and Sunglow—the six top contenders. At the jarring bell, W.M. Goetz's Your Host, the favorite with Johnny Longden up, took the lead over the fast track as expected—he was "unratable." On the far turn it was still Your Host now followed by Middleground who was never far back and catching up fast. At the top of the stretch, Your Host faded badly and Middleground took command. Hill Prince, who had been crowded in the far turn, ran gamely but was interfered with by the tiring Your Host. He cleared Your Host and still came on but couldn't catch Middleground who flew under the wire one-and-a-half lengths ahead of his pursuer.

Max Hirsch had himself a third Derby win. He said of Middleground's win over Hill Prince that it gave him the most pleasure of the three as everyone likes to win when he isn't supposed to. He had taken a gamble, releasing Arcaro from his horse so that he could ride Hill Prince, and had given the ride to his young apprentice, Billy Boland. Boland rode a great race. Middleground won the Belmont and came second in the Preakness.

Until his death in 1969 at the age of 89, Hirsch was still rising at dawn in the cottage next to Barn I at Belmont to oversee the King Ranch horses as he had done for 50 years. As a boy in Texas he could recall "unfriendly Indians." At ten he went to work for John Morris riding quarter horses and then stowed away on a freight car bound for Morris' thoroughbred farm in Maryland.

Count Turf ✦ May 5, 1951

Conn McCreary is jubilant on Count Turf, who strikes a handsome stance in the winner's circle. Assistant trainer "Slim" Sully holds the reins with owner "Big Jack" Amiel just behind his arm.

The night before the Derby of 1951, Jack Amiel and his jockey, Conn McCreary, walked into the same restaurant where Eddie Arcaro was dining. Arcaro had the ride on the favorite, Cain Hoy Stable's Battle Morn. Amiel's horse, Count Turf, had suffered the indignation of being lumped in with "the field." Arcaro asked Amiel who he liked for the race and Amiel responded, "Are you kidding? I like my horse." "You're nuts," said Arcaro and went back to his steak.

Trainer Sol Rutchick thought so little of Count Turf's chances he stayed in New York. When he learned McCreary was going to ride he offered to at least get Amiel a good jockey. McCreary had been on a losing streak since his win on Pensive (Derby, 1944), but he had risen to fame as a come-from-behind rider and Count Turf was a come-from-behind kind of horse.

Count Turf arrived by airplane in Louisville, the first Derby horse to do so. Amiel, who operated the Turf Restaurant on Manhattan's Broadway, had never trained a horse, but he would stand near trainers like Max Hirsch at the Downs in the morning, and if Hirsch sent Sonic five furlongs in a certain time, Amiel would instruct McCreary to do the same. McCreary exchanged the Count's chain bit for a simple D ring snaffle, and the horse ran "like a hoop around a barrel."

The Count broke with the first flight and was near the top as they passed the stands. On the backstretch Calumet's Fanfare moved toward the leaders and The Count went with him. At the far turn, McCreary had lost Fanfare and moved on the leader, Repetoire. One of the other jockeys later said, "He sounded like a can opener cutting through the field, clucking and hollering as he picked up holes and shifted his horse back and forth." Count Turf circled Repetoire on the final turn and hightailed it for home. Royal Mustang made a bid for him but just couldn't keep up. "He just galloped," said Amiel. "He win (*sic*) it all by himself."

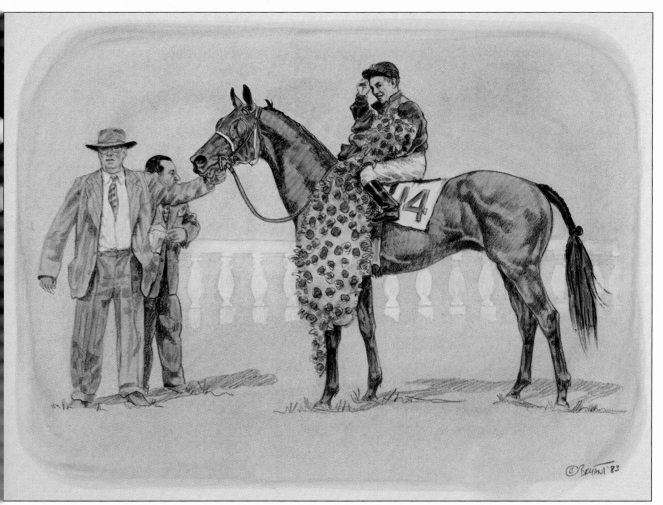

Hill Gail ✦ May 3, 1952

The "Jones Boys"—the inscrutable Ben on the left and son Jimmy on the right—lead Eddie Arcaro on Hill Gail into the 1952 Derby winner's circle.

Hill Gail was high strung like Blenheim II, his dam's sire, and his dam was "a well-authenticated bitch," in the words of Ben Jones, but like his uncle, Whirlaway, he could run like the wind. When Hill Gail became neurotic in the paddock before the race, Ben Jones punched him in the nose. Hill Gail was by Bull Lea, that great Calumet sire who was unplaced in the 1938 Derby but sired Derby winners Citation (1848) and Iron Liege (1957), as well as Coaltown, who was second to Citation.

Jones and Arcaro were together again and the pair would prove unbeatable. The bettors made them the overwhelming favorite at even money over White Oak Stable's Blue Man with Conn McCreary looking for a third win. When the gate opened, Hill Gail got the jump on the field. Hannibal made a bid for him on the first turn but fell away. After that nobody came close. All alone on the backstretch Arcaro sensed that Hill Gail was going to try to duck into the gap for the barn area and he smacked him with his whip. Hill Gail nearly ran away with him. He opened up a six-length lead and outlasted Sub Fleet in a thrilling finish.

Hill Gail's winning time of 2:03⅗ came within one-fifth of a second of Whirlaway's record. It was the sixth win for Ben Jones, putting him at the top of the trainers' list over "Derby Dick" Thompson by two and further out of reach. It was the fifth win for Arcaro and made him the winningest Derby jockey by two over Isaac Murphy and Earl Sande, and it was the fifth as well for Calumet Farm.

Dark Star ✦ *May 2, 1953*

**Eric Guerin in Alfred Vanderbilt's silks on Native Dancer battles for
the lead in the stretch with Dark Star.**

There was no question in anybody's mind who the winner of the 79th Kentucky Derby would be—Native Dancer, Alfred G. Vanderbilt's sensational "Gray Ghost," who had won all his races leading up to the Derby. In 1952, Native Dancer had been proclaimed one of the best two-year-olds of all time, and he was the first of racing's television stars as his three-year career spanned the early years of that industry's growth. After his defeat in the Derby, he won each time out for the remainder of that season and the next. He probably would have won the Derby had he not been bumped in the early going by Money Broker. His reputation has suffered from the stigma of having not won the Derby, the significance of which, in this case, is overrated.

In all fairness to Dark Star, Harry F. Guggenheim's handsome brown colt who had won the Derby Trial, that horse ran a magnificent race. Going to the front in the first quarter, Dark Star never relinquished the lead. Correspondent, with Eddie Arcaro, recovered from an early interference and was closest to Dark Star off the far turn but had nothing left for the drive. Native Dancer had recovered under the expert handling of Eric Guerin who had brought him up to third at the top of the stretch and, passing Correspondent, closed the gap to Dark Star. Hank Moreno went to the whip on the leader and the two horses battled down to the wire. With Native Dancer still gaining and his nose at Dark Star's cheek, they passed the finish.

Alfred Gwynne Vanderbilt struggled through two levels of crowded grandstand and must have run to be the first to congratulate his friend Harry Guggenheim on his win. The two men, though separated by 12 years in age, each represented pinnacles of wealth, social position and sportsmanship in America. Vanderbilt shook his hand and said, "If it had to be anybody, Harry, I'm glad it was you." Native Dancer went on to win, in all, 21 races out of 22 starts, the lone blemish being the 1953 Kentucky Derby.

Determine stretches to touch the nose of Gloire Fille; they were sire and dam, respectively, of 1962 Derby winner, Decidedly.

This Derby was similar to that of the year before in several ways. In 1953 the gray colt, Native Dancer, was bumped in the early going and should have won but didn't. In 1954, the gray colt, Determine, was also bumped in the early going, and shouldn't have won but did. Determine became the first gray horse to win the Kentucky Derby and the first California horse to do so since Morvich in 1922. Although bred in Kentucky, Determine was owned by Californian A.J. Crevolin and campaigned in that state.

Seventeen horses went to the post for this 80th running of the classic, with Correlation favored and Bill Shoemaker in the irons looking for his first of what would be five Derby wins. Arcaro, on Goyamo, was looking for his sixth. The winner of the Derby Trial, Hasty Road, with Adams up, figured to be at the top. Determine, by Alibhai out of Koubis, was a minute 870 pounds, but what he lacked in size he made up for in heart.

As the horses broke from the gate, the 5 to 1 shot, Hasty Road, crossed in front of five horses to bump Timely Tip, who jostled Determine. Though badly roughed, Determine recovered well under Ray York, who kept him off Hasty Road's blistering pace, knowing from the Derby Trial that Hasty Road would burn them out. At the end of the mile, Hasty Road was still on top, but York had moved Determine up to challenge, passing Timely Tip. Determine responded to York's urging at the top of the stretch and passed the tiring Hasty Road. It was all over but the shouting, and there was plenty of that as all the Californians in the place sang and yelled, "California, here I come!" The little gray colt won the country's biggest race by one-and-a-half lengths.

© Bryant '83

Swaps ✦ May 7, 1955

A portrait of Swaps at stud at John Galbreath's Darby Dan Farm (formerly Bradley's Idle Hour) in Lexington, Kentucky.

Since Swaps, one of the favorites, was owned and trained by Mormons, the church would receive ten percent of his earnings. His owners were the Ellsworth Brothers, Rex and Reed, nondrinking Mormon cowpokes who, with $850 in savings from their $50-a-week jobs, rented an old truck and headed for the 1933 Fasig-Tipton Sales in Lexington. There they bought six mares and two weanlings for $600. From this meager stake, Rex became a power in California racing, and in 1946 borrowed $160,000 to buy the stallion, Khaled, from Aly Khan. Khaled sired a dozen stakes winners, one of which was Swaps, who failed to catch much notice at two, although he won three of his six starts, but drew attention in the early part of his next season by wins in the San Vicente Stakes and Santa Anita Derby.

Ellsworth shipped Swaps to Louisville by rail with trainer Mesach Tenney in the same boxcar. At the Downs, Tenney set up residence in Swaps' stall just as Major Barak Thomas had done to protect his favorite, Himyar, the night before the fourth Derby (1878).

On Derby Day, 1955, Swaps and his rider, Willie Shoemaker, had only one real rival—Nashua, with Eddie Arcaro aboard. Swaps quickly got out on the lead, and although Nashua narrowed it to a half-length by the stretch, at the wire it was Swaps, clearly the best by one-and-a-half lengths, eight lengths in front of Summer Tan.

Swaps returned to his home state and picked up several important stakes. But Nashua got his revenge in their match race at the end of the summer, getting off to a quick lead that Swaps was never able to overcome. John Galbreath paid Ellsworth $1 million for half-interest in Swaps when the colt finished racing and a year later his wife put up another $1 million to buy him outright for stud duty at Darby Dan.

Needles winning the Flamingo Stakes. Needles was the first Florida bred to win the Kentucky Derby.

*N*amed Needles because of all the injections he was given to cure his many ailments, the bay foal grew up to win blue ribbons for his conformation as a yearling. He was speedy and precocious at two, setting a track record for four-and-a-half furlongs as early in the year as April. At age three, he began to develop the running style of his father, Ponder, winner of the 1949 Derby. He would wait until the last possible moment in a race before making his move.

In this fashion, Needles clicked off impressive scores in the Flamingo Stakes and the Florida Derby. But he was a big question mark for the Kentucky Derby. It had been six weeks since the colt had had a race or even a decent workout. Then he drew the inside post position, a disadvantage for a stretch runner. His trainer, one-time flying ace Hugh Fontaine, viewed the post position philosophically: "I love it," he said. "I might as well love it, 'cause it's the only one I'm going to get."

Needles was 27 lengths back with a half-mile to go and 15 lengths back when the pack reached "Heartbreak Lane." "When I asked him for it, he just went 'boom'," said the jubilant Dave Erb. "We found an opening at about the three-eighths pole, went outside first, and then in." Weaving through the crowd, Needles had come back for one of the most exciting Derbies ever but was also the slowest winner since his sire, Ponder, sauntered under the wire.

The Kentucky Derby had another "triple": Reigh Count had sired Count Fleet, who sired Count Turf. Pensive sired Ponder, who sired Needles.

Iron Liege ✦ May 4, 1957

Bill Shoemaker on Gallant Man, thinking he had crossed the wire, stands up briefly—giving Bill Hartack on Iron Liege the edge at the wire in the "Bad Dream" Derby.

Iron Liege was a third stringer for Calumet. Their hottest prospect, Barbizon, was two-year-old champion but developed a respiratory condition. So trainer Jimmy Jones trotted out General Duke and Iron Liege as his one-two combination. They finished one and three in the Everglades, two and three in the Flamingo, one and three in the Florida Derby, and one and two in the Fountain of Youth.

For the 83rd running, the smallish field included Bold Ruler, fresh from a track-record performance in the Wood, and the horse he had just nosed out in that race, Gallant Man. The good horse Round Table loomed a sharp foe.

Iron Liege pressed the pace and had his head in front as the field rolled into the stretch. Gallant Man was third, and Shoemaker was driving him. The colt overtook Iron Liege for a moment well up the stretch; however, it was not as far up the stretch as Shoemaker thought. He stood up in the irons, believing that the race was over and he had won. He realized his mistake, but not quickly enough. Bill Hartack shot Iron Liege through to the slimmest kind of victory, the first of five Derby victories for Hartack.

Gallant Man's owner, Ralph Lowe, had dreamed a few nights earlier that "The Shoe" would misjudge the finish. He warned trainer John Nerud and Shoemaker at dinner and, perhaps as a testimony to the power of suggestion, that's just what Shoemaker did.

167

Tim Tam ✦ May 3, 1958

**Tim Tam at stud, with the Calumet barn in the background, looks out alertly.
Mrs. Gene Markey, the owner of Calumet (inset).**

Calumet had developed a rising star in a horse named Kentucky Pride, but when that horse was injured they pulled Tim Tam off the bench. Tim Tam, by Tom Fool, won the Everglades, the Flamingo, the Fountain of Youth and the Florida Derby. He then came north to Keeneland and sped seven panels in track-record time. His final tune-up was in the Derby Trial, which he won in handy fashion.

Tim Tam had beat off a 75 to 1 shot named Lincoln Road in the Florida Derby and had been moved up into first place in the Flamingo on the disqualification of Jewel's Reward. Besides those two horses, Tim Tam also faced Silky Sullivan in the Derby, the California crowd pleaser whose come-from-behind runs were the stuff of legends.

On Derby Day the crowd had installed Jewel's Reward as the slight favorite over Tim Tam and Silky Sullivan. Silky, who had won races after having trailed by as many as 25 lengths, couldn't handle a muddy track, and Jewel's Reward ended up running an even race for fourth. The real contest was between Tim Tam and Lincoln Road. Lincoln Road led the entire race, except for the last few critical yards. Tim Tam, ranging out from the middle of the pack under a long consistent drive, wore down his game rival for a half-length victory.

Tim Tam and his jockey, Ismael Valenzuela, scored a more decisive victory over Lincoln Road in the Preakness. Then in the Belmont he shattered a sesamoid bone at the quarter pole, yet still managed to hold on for second place. But his career was over. He would have been Calumet's third Triple Crown winner.

Tomy Lee ✦ May 2, 1959

Tomy Lee, with Bill Shoemaker, gets a lead from trainer Frank Childs.

Texas oilman Fred Turner, Jr., figuring that somebody had already named a horse "Tommy Lee," came up with his own novel spelling. Tomy Lee was bred in England and purchased by Turner as an afterthought. He had just spent $25,000 on a more fashionably bred colt and wanted the horse to have a companion for the long trek to the States. So he picked up Tomy Lee for $6,762. His high-priced colt earned back half his sales tag before an injury brought on retirement. Tomy Lee was to go on to repay his purchase price 60 times over.

At two, Tomy won six tries in California then traveled east to lose two tough contests to First Landing. At three he came up short in his early West Coast starts, but was undefeated in the East. The striking-looking colt came up to the Derby with two impressive victories at Keeneland: a track record for seven furlongs in the first and then he won the Blue Grass Stakes. In the Derby, his old rival, First Landing, went off as the slight favorite.

Tomy Lee, with Willie Shoemaker in the irons, put in a tough fight to gain the lead but surrendered it to Sword Dancer with a quarter-of-a-mile to go. As they rounded the turn for home, Tomy Lee, on the rail, drew even with Sword Dancer but carried him wide on the turn. As they battled through the stretch, Sword Dancer lugged back in but just failed to outlast Tomy Lee. Sword Dancer's jockey claimed foul but it was disallowed by the stewards. In this his second Derby win, "Shoe" made up for his ride in the "Bad Dream" Derby.

Tomy Lee was retired at the end of the year, but had difficulty getting mares in foal, so at six he was sent back to the track. He picked up four more winner's checks before resuming the life of leisure as a stallion.

Venetian Way ✦ May 7, 1960

Venetian Way jogs out onto the foggy track for an early morning gallop.

The damp crowd of 75,000 fancied Tompion, at practically even money, due to a four-race win record that included the Santa Anita Derby and the Blue Grass Stakes. Also popular at the pari-mutuels was Bally Ache, who had defeated the third favorite, Venetian Way, in three out of four of their encounters, including a seven-furlong prep at Churchill Downs several days before the Derby.

In the 86th running, Venetian Way was third after five furlongs, second with a quarter-mile to go, first at the top of the stretch and first where it counted the most. His time of 2:02 2/5 was the fastest Derby run on an "off" track. Sports writer Red Smith compared the track condition that day to "used eating tobacco."

Especially warmed by the victory of this game colt were owner Isaac Blumberg and trainer Vic Sovinski. They had campaigned the good colt Lincoln Road in 1958 but kept running into Tim Tam. Said Sovinski, "I would rather win the Kentucky Derby than any other race in the world and I don't care if I never win another race." This was the second of five Derby wins for jockey Bill Hartack.

**Carry Back and jockey John Sellers, in the blue and silver silks of
Mrs. Katherine Price, at the 16th pole.**

*H*orses that perfect a late rush that gets them to the wire just in time tend to be big favorites with the public. Fans are also taken with honest hard-knocking horses. The public also likes a Cinderella story, where a bargain-basement horse rises up to beat his better-bred rivals. Carry Back was a born crowd pleaser.

His owner/trainer, Jack Price, was a new breed of horseman and his colt came from Ocala, Florida, a new center of the thoroughbred breeding industry. The horse that Jack Price bred for a $400 stud fee to a nonwinning mare bought for $265, raced a grueling 21 times as a freshman. Carry Back set a couple of track records that year and came from off the pace to win such important fixtures as the Cowdin, the Garden State and the Remsen.

Carry Back developed into the people's horse through his stirring contests with Crozier in the rich Florida winter stakes. On Derby Day, the betting public took a good look at Crozier, who had just sped to a Churchill Downs track record earlier that week in the Derby Trial. But they made Carry Back the favorite, his support coming largely from the $2 bets of the infield multitudes.

Carry Back gave the fans just what they had packed the Downs to see. At the quarter pole he was 13 lengths back, but coming into the stretch he was fourth, trailing Crozier by six lengths. Then John Sellers let him all the way out and it was all over for the speedy Crozier as Carry Back drove fans wild with an almost two-length win.

Carry Back won the Preakness, but was upset in the Belmont. He'd be back to battle the best of his era, though, for years to come, and a career total of $1,226,665. He was racing's second millionaire, the first since Citation.

Decidedly ✦ *May 5, 1962*

The beautiful head of Decidedly with trainer Horatio Luro.

O n the basis of his record, Decidedly had little going for him, but he was the son of 1954 Derby winner Determine. In addition he was bred by Californian George Pope, Jr., of the noted El Peco Ranch, trained by the sage Argentinian, Horatio Luro, and ridden by Bill Hartack.

The *Blood-Horse* filed this report on the 1962 Derby: "It was not only the fastest Derby in the race's 88-year history, it was one of the most exciting. The time of 2:00⅖ was a full second better than Whirlaway's record which had stood since 1941. During the hectic mile-and-a-quarter, the lead changed from the outsider Lee Town to Sunrise Country to Admiral's Voyage to Roman Line before the gray Decidedly found an opening to the outside at the eighth pole. From then on, with Bill Hartack riding hard, the gray moved two-and-a-quarter lengths clear of Roman Line." Decidedly was the second gray to win the classic. The first was his sire, Determine.

For Hartack, it was Derby win number three. He was the Bobby Fischer of racing, blunt to the point of rudeness. Born in poverty as the son of a coal miner, he'd worked his way to the top by tooth and nail. "Hatred is necessary for my work," he once explained to a reporter. "The madder I get, the better I ride." Tying Eddie Arcaro's record with five wins, it took Arcaro 21 tries Hartack did it in nine. The best riding average is still Winkfield's with his two wins, one second and one third in four attempts.

Chateaugay ✦ May 4, 1963

A thorn from the rose blanket jabs Chateaugay, who never needed an excuse to "act up."
Braulio Baeza sits coolly and owner John Galbreath left, holds the roses.

The mint julep is the Derby's official drink and julep toasts were being drunk to the expected Derby winner long before the race was run and were still being drunk to a son of Swaps named Chateaugay long after the last race was over.

Chateaugay had looked sharp winning the Blue Grass Stakes a few weeks earlier, but the crowd had two undefeated horses to consider, so this sleek chestnut paid a respectable $20.80 to his backers. Jockey Braulio Baeza, the Panamanian sensation, timed his charge perfectly from the middle of the pack and wore down the tiring leaders. It was the first Derby win for owner-breeder John W. Galbreath, trainer J.P. Conway and Baeza.

Chateaugay carried a little good luck with him in the race. Galbreath's cook sent along a few chicken wishbones, and the millionaire owner dutifully fastened them to his horse's saddle before sending Chateaugay out to victory.

Northern Dancer ✦ *May 2, 1964*

Canadian owner E.P. Taylor holds Northern Dancer with Bill Hartack up.
Trainer Horatio Luro is on the left of Taylor.

*A*s the field rounded the stretch for home, the second favorite, Northern Dancer, was still in the lead after clocking swift fractions with Bill Hartack in the irons. Moving quickly through the pack was the favored Hill Rise with Shoemaker aboard. Hill Rise was in the process of running the fastest final quarter-mile in Derby history as he pulled even with the leader. But the race was probably won when Hartack moved decisively with Northern Dancer at the five-furlong pole, taking Shoemaker and Hill Rise by surprise. The two horses had been running side by side behind a wall of three horses. Hartack eased Northern Dancer away from the rail and they spurted to the outside in front of Hill Rise. Shoemaker later said that he could not get his big horse moving in time to prevent Northern Dancer's nimble escape.

Northern Dancer edged the favored Hill Rise in the record time of 2:00 flat. His Derby win was the first for a Canadian bred and for breeder E.P. Taylor. It was the second time around for trainer Horatio Luro, whose Decidedly had smashed all previous Derby records in 1962. Now Luro broke that time by two-fifths of a second with Northern Dancer.

Northern Dancer won three major Derby prep races—the Flamingo, Florida Derby and Blue Grass—on his way to Churchill Downs. After running for the roses, he picked up the black-eyed Susans of the Preakness and then won the most important Canadian classic, the Queen's Plate. He is best known for his success as a sire and for the astronomical prices his yearlings fetched.

All alone in midstretch, although they would be challenged imminently, are Lucky Debonair and Bill Shoemaker in Ada L. Rice's colors. Inset: Bill Shoemaker.

Frank Catrone, a short, portly man, was one of a few trainers to face the 4' 11" Bill Shoemaker on even terms. Lucky Debonair, the Vertex colt out of a Count Fleet mare, had won the Santa Anita Derby and the Blue Grass Stakes at one-and-an-eighth miles (the perfect "prep" distance to the Derby) by slim margins. No one realized that, once on the lead, Lucky Debonair would try to pull himself up. He always had energy to spare, but Tom Rolfe and Bold Lad were favored for this Derby.

Flag Raiser took the lead past the stands, with Lucky Debonair two lengths back. Johnny Rotz on Native Charger thought he was sitting "in the golden chair" coming up the backstretch behind Flag Raiser with Bold Lad sixth and Dapper Dan dead last. Flag Raiser, still on the lead coming out of the far turn started to tire and Lucky Debonair took command. Ron Turcotte, in his first Derby appearance, on Tom Rolfe, tried to slip through on the rail inside Flag Raiser, but Bobby Ussery closed them off. In midstretch Lucky Debonair was all alone and could have coasted, but then came Dapper Dan from last place to challenge him in the final dash. A chestnut son of Ribot, Dapper Dan had looped the field and was still gaining on the leader when they passed under the wire with Lucky Debonair clinging to his lead by a neck. Tom Rolfe was third and Bold Lad, the victim of leg problems, beat only one horse of the 11.

Kauai King ◆ May 7, 1966

Groom "Popeye" Stevenson leads the son of Native Dancer in a victory procession from the winner's circle at the 92nd Kentucky Derby. "It's the biggest day of my life!" exclaimed Popeye.

On a warm and "fast-track" day, the son of Native Dancer, who was unbeaten in 22 starts except for the Derby, avenged his father's defeat of 1953 and did it leading from wire to wire. Although Kauai King was slightly favored, his colors were unfamiliar to the crowd of over 100,000, as was the jockey, Donald Brumfield. Brumfield was one of the best at rating a horse on the lead but was known only in Louisville where he had raced over the Churchill Downs oval hundreds of times.

It had all the appearances of being a boring Derby. Overshadowed by the absence of Graustark, who was injured, the 15 remaining horses seemed to be leftovers of what had been a good crop of three-year-olds. No one expected the thrilling race it became, least of all Kauai King's owner, Mike Ford, who had only been in the racing game six years. But he and trainer Henry Forrest believed in the colt they had brought along: Kauai King had won six of his last eight times out.

No one else in the classic ever really had a chance. At the bell, Kauai King broke so well from the gate he was on top by the first turn. They sizzled, the first quarter in :22⅘. When they covered the mile in 1:35, it looked like it was all over for the King: Horses just don't do a mile in the Derby in that time and still hang on to win. John Sellers drove Advocator in hot pursuit, nearly catching Kauai King at the quarter pole. Abe's Hope, with Shoemaker, made a spectacular run circling the field on the turn but faded abruptly at the top of the stretch. Stupendous attempted to come alongside with Blue Skyer, but while Blue Skyer held on to just miss the roses by a nose, Stupendous gave up the ghost.

Don Brumfield said to himself as he came down the stretch, whipping and pumping, with everyone in the race taking a shot at them, "Help me Lord, 'cause I need you now," but the veteran Kentucky jockey didn't need a hand on this day that made him the "happiest hillbilly hardboot you've ever seen! As he tossed his whip to his groom, "Popeye," he spoke for Kauai King as well when he said to Henry Forrest, "Thank you, Papa."

© BRYANT '83

"FORWARD PASS - DANCERS IMAGE" MAY 4, 1968

189

Majestic Prince ✦ May 3, 1969

Bill Hartack sits on Majestic Prince as he is weighed before the Belmont Stakes.

The story of the 95th Derby is that of Johnny Longden and the horse he trained and exercised himself. The spectacular-looking chestnut colt by Raise a Native was unbeaten and favored to win. The ex-jockey kept him supplied with his favorite peppermint candy.

As the race got underway, Top Knight faded suddenly and was overtaken by Paul Mellon's Arts and Letters. Bill Hartack watched Arts and Letters go by, then roused "The Prince." Majestic Prince caught and passed Arts and Letters at the eighth pole, but Arts and Letters, with Braulio Baeza, hung on and dueled down to the wire with Dike, who had come from out of nowhere. All three passed under the wire together, with Majestic Prince in front by only a neck. Longden became the first man to win the Kentucky Derby both as a jockey (Count Fleet, 1943) and as a trainer. Bill Hartack tied Eddie Arcaro for the most wins of a jockey.

Majestic Prince went on to win the Preakness, but after that effort was so exhausted "he jus' sleep and sleep," his groom said. Longden argued with owner Frank McMahon not to run him in the Belmont. The horse had "corded up" after the Preakness, and his flanks were sunken. He had lost over 40 pounds. "Something has been said about me being a quitter," said McMahon, and he insisted that the horse run—to Longden's despair. Majestic Prince ran a game race to finish second to Arts and Letters, his old foe, and lost the Triple Crown. Then he developed leg troubles and, as Longden predicted, never ran again. The horse whose star had risen so quickly was ruined. Majestic Prince was not the first victim of the Triple Crown: Old Rosebud didn't recover until two years after the Derby, Canonero II was lame for a year after his efforts and Dancer's Image was through after the Derby and Preakness.

Dust Commander ✦ May 2, 1970

Dust Commander sniffs inquisitively at Mike Manganello's bouquet of roses. A guard in the background savors his single bud.

The 96th Derby was a "blessed event" for Dust Commander and Mike Manganello. Archbishop Emmanuel Milingo of Zambia had stepped in front of the horse as he paraded in the Keeneland paddock before the Blue Grass Stakes and performed the usual blessing for domestic animals. Then he went to the window and bet $2 across the board on the little colt by Bold Commander (by Bold Ruler). The archbishop was not there by accident but as a guest of the owners.

The heretofore unnoticed colt Robert Lehmann had bought as a yearling for $6,500 easily trounced Corn off the Cob and the Blue Grass field and paid 35 to 1. Lehmann who was on the border of India and Nepal tracking "big game" at the time, flew 70 hours to see Dust Commander run in the Derby.

Archbishop Milingo couldn't be at the Derby and when Mrs. Lehmann asked if he shouldn't bless the horse again, the archbishop informed her that "when a horse is blessed he is blessed"; however, he did have a premonition involving a number four horse.

Mike Manganello was not a big-name Northern jockey, but he had ridden the Louisville track hundreds of times. So when he and Dust Commander were badly roughed up at the start, he maneuvered his nimble colt to the inside rail where they hung saving ground. At the half-mile pole he let Dust Commander start to pick up horses by himself but going into the last turn a sigh went up from the crowd: not Dust Commander but the number four horse, Holy Land of all names, had gone down. Diane Crump, the first woman to ride in the Derby, was not involved, but Hector Pilar lay motionless. Manganello swung Dust Commander wide in the homestretch and took the lead. Hector Pilar survived his back injuries and the archbishop of Zambia took home $1,662.60 for the Zambia Helper's Society.

193

Canonero II ✦ May 1, 1971

Owner Pedro Baptista and Canonero II after the colt's win in the 97th Derby.

A month before the Kentucky Derby, the heavily favored Hoist the Flag broke his leg in a workout at Belmont Park. He was saved for stud duty by the genius of equine surgeon Jacques Jenny and the Derby was wide open. The accident was devastating to owner Jane Clark and trainer Sidney Watters, of Middleburg, Virginia. But what was a tragedy for the famous horse became a Cinderella story for the unknown.

Juan Arias was raised in the slums of Caracas, Venezuela, but he attended a four-year government school for horse trainers. American-bred Canonero, was born with a foreleg that bent backward from the knee. The unsightly blemish kept buyers away, despite his Pretendre-Dixieland II breeding, and he sold for $1,200 to Venezuelan industrialist Pedro Bautista. He moved like a crab, but he won his first outing in Venezuela by six-and-a-half lengths.

No one in the States had heard of Canonero II or knew that he won in Venezuela at the Derby distance two months prior, not only in deep sand but also at an altitude of 3,000 feet. When the Canonero entourage arrived at Churchill Downs they were shunned by the racing establishment. Arias would work his horse any time of the day, and often lead him with a rope around his neck. He was not invited to the pre-Derby dinner for trainers and Canonero was lumped in with the "field" at 9 to 1.

The tension in Canonero's saddling stall was unbearable. Arias' hands were shaking so hard he couldn't tighten the girth without help. Robert Kleberg of King Ranch watched the unknown South American colt and commented that he was about the best-looking he'd ever seen.

Canonero got off to a bad start, 15th in the field of 20, but opened up on the far turn and, with Gustavo Avila whipping like a windmill, looped the field and won by three-and-a-half lengths. Silence blanketed the grandstand. "Canonero II," exclaimed a reporter. "Who the hell was Canonero I?"

Canonero went on to win the Preakness and the country was his. Offered $3 million if Canonero won the Triple Crown, Baptist ran the tired colt in the Belmont against Arias's objections. He ran fourth and sold to the sagacious Kleburg for $1.5 million.

Penny Tweedy gives Riva Ridge a congratulatory pat in the winner's circle.

*I*n 1936 Christopher Chenery bought the old family homestead in Doswell, Virginia, where he had spent his boyhood summers. The 2,600-acre "Meadow" became the nursery for 41 stakes winners, among them Hill Prince, First Landing, Cicada, Riva Ridge and Secretariat. When Chenery was hospitalized in 1967, his daughter, Penny, took over The Meadow, determined to keep the blue and white blocks of her father's silks flying.

By Riva's two-year-old spring, Penny knew she had something when she wrote in her stable log, "The boys like. Will be a racehorse." Penny chose trainer Roger Laurin, son of Canadian trainer Lucien Laurin, but when Ogden Phipps' trainer died in 1971 Roger went to work for him and recommended his father to Mrs. Tweedy. They hit it off immediately. Lucien enlisted the Canadian champion jockey Ron Turcotte, and with Ed Sweat and Charlie Davis as groom and exercise rider, the team was formed.

That summer, Lucien Laurin sent Riva out to work with the four-year-old speedster Three Martinis to "move him up a bit." He told the boy on Three Martinis to stay back with Riva and not "break" him. As the two were flying down the track, Charlie Davis on Riva said to the other, "The man wants this horse to work. Let your horse out!" The other replied, "I can't pick him up and carry him!" Lucien then knew he had a superhorse. Riva broke the world record for one-and-three-sixteenth miles that year in 1:52⅖ and earned over $503,000 as the new two-year-old champion.

After a long rest in Florida, he came up to the Derby in perfect shape mentally and physically despite his loss in the "Everglades," where he was trapped on the rail. He won the Blue Grass and in the Derby broke from the number nine slot and headed straight for the lead. When Marquez, on Hold Your Peace, made a move to test him, Riva and Turcotte took a length lead. When Marquez moved up again at the far turn, Riva spurted away and led the field by three lengths coming into the homestretch. No Le Hace came on but could not catch him. From his hospital room in New York, Chris Chenery watched his daughter on television clutch the gold trophy. Riva had won for him and for The Meadow.

Secretariat ✦ *May 5, 1973*

Oil Painting of "Big Red" coming straight on with an intensity and power unequaled in modern times

Secretariat captured the Triple Crown in 1973 and was the first horse to do so since Citation 25 years earlier.

"Wow!" exclaimed Penny Tweedy when she first saw the chestnut foal by Bold Ruler out of Somethingroyal. Lucien was afraid he was too good looking to really run but Secretariat won eight races straight as a two-year-old. Before his first start at three he was syndicated for over $6 million.

Secretariat became a TV star, the first racehorse with a Nielsen rating, and his handsome face graced the covers of *Time*, *Newsweek* and *Sports Illustrated*. Aloof and self-contained in the paddock, last from the gate as usual, but he gathered steam like a locomotive. The powerful haunches collected then propelled him forward in earth-eating strides. At the end of the clubhouse turn he finally fired and blasted up the backstretch, gobbling all in his way. Up front, Sham passed Shecky Greene on the last turn and as they straightened out for the stretch there was Secretariat alongside. It was a two-horse race. Sham, his mouth bleeding heavily from an accident in the gate, held on gamely but could not outstay "Big Red." Secretariat's individual fractions were :25⅕, :24¼, :23⅗, and :23. He ran each quarter-mile faster than the one before and beat Northern Dancer's 1964 record by three-fifths of a second. It was Ron Turcotte's second Derby win in a row.

Secretariat repeated his performance in the Preakness and in the Belmont he barged down the stretch 31 lengths ahead. He took a full 2⅗ seconds off Gallant Man's 1957 record.

Poor Riva Ridge. His own brilliant Derby victory eclipsed and his $1 million career forgotten, he turned his rump to his stall opening when the crowds gathered around Secretariat's stall next door. In the only time they ever met on the track, both Riva and his stablemate broke the world record for one-and-one-eighth miles in the Marlboro Cup, but Secretariat won by three-and-a-half lengths over Riva. Riva was a great horse, unfortunately overshadowed by one greater.

Cannonade ✦ *May 4, 1974*

Trainer Woody Stephens on a lead pony takes Cannonade and Angel Cordero out for a morning spin.

It was the 100th year of the Kentucky Derby. A century of fine racing at the Louisville racetrack was uninterrupted by two world wars—even the Great Depression only delayed the Derby of 1929 by a month. John Olin's Cannonade, trained by Woody Stephens and ridden by the Puerto Rican jockey Angel Cordero, won this centennial Derby in the unspectacular time of 2:05 over a fast track. What was spectacular was the event. All previous attendance records were shattered by 30,000. The winner won more money ($274,000), the bettors handed over more money ($3,444,649 on the Derby alone), and everyone in the infield had more fun than any previous year. Police were helpless to prevent the hordes from hanging on the inside rail. They were unable to chase a band of half-naked youths from the top of one of the toteboards or to catch any of the streakers who ran amok. Princess Margaret, the Queen of England's fun-loving sister, said it was a lovely day of racing in the country. She donated a special jeweled cup to the winner. More horses by one than Reigh Count's record field of 23 went to the post, half of them shouldn't have been there. It was a horse from the field, Hudson County, who set the pace and held on for place money.

At the end of "God Save the Queen," "The Stars and Stripes Forever" and "My Old Kentucky Home," the gates loosed a phalanx of charging, color-splashed equines. There was a lot of bumping and knocking. Shoemaker on Agitate was shaken up and trapped on the rail, but Cordero dodged and scooted Cannonade through holes all the way, catching Hudson County then leaving him by four lengths at the eighth pole and going on to win by the same margin. Of his video-game-like ride through the traffic, Cordero said, "It was a beautiful trip."

<h1 style="text-align: center;">*Foolish Pleasure* ✦ *May 3, 1975*</h1>

John Greer leads Jacinto Vasquez on Foolish Pleasure past the tulips to the winner's circle.

Foolish Pleasure put to rest any doubts as to his true quality when he triumphed in a spectacular manner in the 101st Kentucky Derby. Seventy-seven-year-old John Greer was delighted with his check for $209,000 and reminded everyone of his horse's hard-fought win in the Wood.

The grandson of Bold Ruler and Tom Fool had distinguished himself as a two-year-old by winning all seven of his outings. In this race he was the third Florida bred (after Needles and Carry Back) to take the Kentucky crown jewel. The favored Avatar and Diabolo from the "Coast" were relegated to second and third and Bombay Duck, who gave him a problem in the Wood, finished last.

Jacinto Vasquez kept Foolish Pleasure off the pace until Bombay Duck faded on the far turn and Avatar and Master Derby took control. With a tremendous surge of speed, Foolish Pleasure drove between the two horses at the head of the stretch just in time to avoid the collision when Diabolo came in on Avatar. Avatar was knocked sideways but gamely managed to finish second. There was a steward's inquiry but both jockeys of the California horses said that they couldn't have caught Foolish Pleasure.

Chick Anderson, announcing the stretch duel, got so excited he called Prince Thou Art in front instead of Foolish Pleasure, which sounded good to Braulio Baeza in sixth on Prince Thou Art but did not in the least deter Vasquez who thought, "I don't know where you are, Baeza, but I'm here at the wire winning this race."

Three months later a match race was set between Foolish Pleasure, the colt of the year, and Ruffian, the filly of the year. This unnatural contest was viewed by millions, who were then treated to the gruesome spectacle of a brilliant filly snapping a leg. Foolish Pleasure had got the jump on the black filly by a head coming out of the gate, but she had rallied and was leading him halfway up the back stretch. The crowd held its collective breath. There were going too fast. Then Ruffian bobbled, ran on her broken hind leg for a few strides and stopped. All efforts to save her were unsuccessful and she was buried in the infield of Belmont Park.

In 1994 Foolish Pleasure, the 11th all-time money winner who sired 37 stakes winners, died from colic at the age of 22 while pasture-breeding mares in Wyoming.

Bold Forbes ✦ May 1, 1976

Angel Cordero on Bold Forbes is led into the winner's circle by trainer Lazaro Barrera.

*I*t's a long way from the backstretch of El Commandante Racetrack in Puerto Rico to the finish line of the Kentucky Derby, but that's where winning horse and rider got their starts. Completing the Latin American lock on the 1976 Derby was the trainer who saddled his first winner at Oriental Park in Havana, Cuba.

Angel Cordero was born on the racetrack. Both grandfathers were jockeys and his father, Angel Cordero, Sr., was probably the greatest rider from Puerto Rico—until Junior came along. The younger Cordero picked up three months' worth of suspensions his first year, but he was still the year's top rider at El Commandante.

Bold Forbes was bred in the blue grass but was sent to Puerto Rico to be broken and trained by the Ubarris, the island's first family of the thoroughbred sport. He was quick to outclass his competition there, and he was shipped back to the States where he won a couple of freshman stakes on the tough New York circuit. At three, he tuned up with a win in a sprint, thought to be his best distance. He then successfully stretched out to a mile-and-an-eighth in the Wood.

Bold Forbes was trained by Hall of Fame trainer Laz Barrera, one of the many Cuban Barrera brothers and sons successfully plying the training trade at American tracks. He took the speedy grandson of Bold Ruler to Kentucky to face the heavily favored Honest Pleasure in the 102nd running of the Derby. Cordero drove "the Puerto Rican Cadillac" to a dramatic upset victory by using his colt's speed to get to the front, and there he stayed, putting away a fierce challenge from Honest Pleasure. Sometime after this his second Derby victory, Cordero returned to Puerto Rico and placed the blanket of roses on his father's grave.

Bold Forbes and Honest Pleasure hooked in a speed duel in the Preakness that burned them both out. In the Belmont, Bold Forbes did what no sprinter should be able to do—last a mile-and-a-half. Cordero got the colt out so far and so fast that he was able to hold on for the win, even though he practically crawled across the finish line. Bold Forbes was named the three-year-old champion of 1976 and helped his trainer earn an Eclipse Award.

Oil painting of Seattle Slew with Jean Cruquet "sitting chilly" as they go into the first turn. (In the collection of Governor Hugh Carey.)

"Well above average in size, shiny coat, bright, alert . . . a well-developed shoulder . . . a good spring of ribs (lots of room for heart and lungs) . . . out in the right foreleg . . . free of worms." That was the auction company's modest assessment of Seattle Slew. The bidding started at $3,000 and 90 seconds later the gavel came down at $17,000. Slew was bought by Mickey Taylor, a Washington lumberman, who took the advice of veterinarian Dr. Jim Hill to bid for Seattle Slew. Hill and his wife became partners with Taylor and his wife in Slew and a handful of other horses. A gawky colt, Slew soon picked up the nickname Baby Huey, after the cartoon character who is always doing everything wrong. But his trainer, Billy Turner, an ex-steeplechase rider, took his time with the colt, not starting him until September of his freshman season. Seattle Slew's three consecutive wins that year included the Champagne Stakes, and it was enough to land him the two-year-old championship. At three, Seattle Slew took major Derby preps in the North and South—the Flamingo Stakes and the Wood Memorial.

The "Slew Crew" of nine—the Taylors, the Hills, the Turners and assorted friends—all arrived in one car on Derby Day. "Huey has all the dignity and the rest of us come up short," said Mrs. Turner. Slew, piloted by the veteran French jockey, Jean Cruget, overcame a bumpy start and was rushed into contention. Squeezing through the pack, he dueled with For a Moment for the lead and then put them all away with a quarter-mile left to run.

The Kentucky Derby was step number one in Seattle Slew's trip to the Triple Crown. He was the first undefeated horse to do so. Slew was also named both three-year-old champion and horse of the year in 1977 and top handicap horse in 1978.

207

Affirmed looks nonchalant in the winner's circle of the 1978 Kentucky Derby. Eighteen-year-old "Stevie" Cauthen grins in this double oil portrait. (In the collection of Ms. Monique Yazigi.)

The 104th Kentucky Derby had all the ingredients of a great contest. There was the East versus the West. It had age and tradition versus youth and progress. Both favorites had met before and each had beaten the other.

On one hand, there was Calumet Farm's outstanding colt, Alydar, the son of Raise a Native. Alydar was the first outstanding Derby prospect for Calumet since Forward Pass' victory ten years earlier. On the other side was Harbor View Farm's Affirmed, a chestnut colt by Exclusive Native. Both these horses had won their last four races with impressive showings. They had met before as two-year-olds and were split, four wins for Affirmed and two for Alydar. On Derby Day, Alydar went off as the 6 to 5 favorite—the odds on Affirmed were 9 to 5.

The race was an exciting, classic duel between two brilliant colts. After the break, Affirmed, running easily, kept with the leaders for the first mile. Alydar was held back, but started to move up at the mile. As the leaders hit the stretch it was Affirmed first, Believe It second and a fast-closing Alydar third. At the wire it was Affirmed by one-and-a-half lengths over Alydar second and Believe It third.

Affirmed went on to win both the Preakness and the Belmont to become American racing's 11th Triple crown winner, the third in a short five-year span that began with Secretariat in 1973, continued with Seattle Slew in 1977 and ended with Affirmed in 1978. They were the superstars of the 1970s. It should not be omitted that Affirmed also helped focus the national spotlight on Steve Cauthen, the 18-year-old Kentucky boy who piloted Affirmed so brilliantly. Trainer Laz Barrera mused that Cauthen probably didn't come from Kentucky at all but from a spaceship, for he had the wisdom of the ages, the finesse of Arcaro and the hands of Shoemaker.

Spectacular Bid ✦ May 5, 1979

**_In this oil painting Spectacular Bid avenges his loss to Coastal in the Belmont Stakes
by beating him here in the Marlboro Cup. (In the collection of Sanford Bryant.)_**

The 1979 Kentucky Derby had been touted as a contest between Flying Paster and Spectacular Bid, both highly regarded horses on winning streaks. The difference would be told, it was thought, by the greater experience of 42-year-old Donald Pierce on Flying Paster. The pressure on Spectacular Bid's teenage jockey, Ronnie Franklin, was almost unbearable. Wisely trainer Bud Delp helped him get a ride on Seethreepeo in the $25,000 Twin Spires, the race immediately preceding the Derby, which they won.

As the gates opened for the Derby, Spectacular Bid stalled and the crowd prepared to blame Franklin. Two days before the race, rain had deluged Churchill Downs. The mud packed in the horses' hooves and the clods thrown back discouraged the best of them. Flying Paster, the second favorite, appeared to scramble, and Screen King, the third favorite, seemed to jump up and down. Ronnie took his big roan horse wide around the pack and it was clear sailing to the wire.

It was "Bid's" 11th straight victory for owners Harry and Teresa Meyerhoff and a vindication for Franklin, who would ride him again on his home ground, Pimlico Race Track, in the Preakness and triumph one more time. Still the doubters encouraged Bud Delp to take Franklin off Spectacular Bid for the Belmont Stakes, third leg of the Triple Crown. Delp refused, keeping faith in the young jockey who was like a son to him. In the Belmont, Bid went straight to the front, uncharacteristically, as if under instructions to set a record. William Haggin Perry's Coastal, who had been campaigned lightly and probably saved for this occasion, wore down the Kentucky Derby winner and won.

Although Bid came out of the race sore, and a stray bandage pin that had stuck in his foot the day of the race was blamed for his defeat, Franklin was removed for the Spectacular Bid/Coastal rematch in the Marlboro Cup. Bid won it handily with the veteran Bill Shoemaker aboard.

211

Genuine Risk ✦ May 3, 1980

**An oil portrait of Genuine Risk in the stretch of the 106th Kentucky Derby.
(In the collection of James L. Kerr.)**

Not since Harry Payne Whitney's Regret in 1915 had a filly won the Kentucky Derby. Genuine Risk was undefeated going into the Wood Memorial, the important prep race six weeks before the Derby; however, in this her first try against the colts, she'd finished third to Plugged Nickle, a Derby candidate in a slow time. The mare was listless and off her feed after the race. Sixteen-year-old Matthew Firestone, who had selected Genuine Risk at the Fasig-Tipton sales, was discouraged. The Derby distance so early in the year is stressful for colts and much more so for the slightly-built fillies, a reason they are given a five-pound weight allowance at that time. Although fillies have won many of France's great classic, the Arc de Triomphe, it is run in October of their third year. Genuine Risk was slight even for a filly.

Genuine Risk was not entered in the Blue Grass Stakes, the final Derby prep, but stepped out onto the track that morning for her first time since the Wood. Jacinto Vasquez said she nearly pulled his arms out. Trainer Leroy Jolley later watched the Blue Grass and when Rockhill Native won in roughly the same slow time Plugged Nickle had won the Wood, and Prince Valiant, who had figured strongly, straggled home last, he realized his mare had a shot at the Derby. As he suspected, eight trainers scratched their horses from the Derby in the wake of the Blue Grass and the field was reduced to 12.

All fears and reservations were laid aside when Genuine Risk barreled past Plugged Nickle and Rockhill Native on the turn for home. Then Bert and Diana Firestone's gallant chestnut filly with the diminutive frame beat off Rumbo's late bid at the wire.

Her next appearance would be at Pimlico in the Preakness. It was just possible that in this year when there were no outstanding colts a filly might actually win the Triple Crown. But Genuine Risk and Vasquez, making their stretch run, were bumped and ridden out by Codex and Angel Cordero who slashed at the filly's head injuring her eye, as the country watched this obvious foul that dashed all hopes for a filly Triple Crown champ.

Pleasant Colony ✦ May 2, 1981

In this oil panting Pleasant Colony blasts down the stretch toward victory with Jorge Velasquez, who would finally receive world recognition for his consistent winning career. (In the collection of John P. Campo.)

Derby officials had invoked a limit on the number of starters in the race which would have left Larry Barrera's Flying Nashua in his stall, and not in the starting gate at Derby time. A court order got Flying Nashua into the race.

The day belonged to the team of Evans, Campo, Valesquez and Pleasant Colony. In the paddock they appeared an unlikely combination: Thomas Mellon Evans, the owner, was a dignified industrialist; John Campo, the trainer, was called the "Fat Man, by Damon Runyon out of a Don Rickles mare"; Jorge Velaquez, the jockey, was a quiet Panamanian and one of the best riders in the country; and finally there was Pleasant Colony, lop-eared, gawky and sporting a nasty-looking skin condition on a hindquarter. He came to Churchill Downs fresh from an upset win in the Wood, where favored Cure the Blues and Proud Appeal had met each other in a speed duel that finished them both. The press latched onto the colorful Campo and gave him numerous opportunities to predict Derby victory to a national audience.

With 21 starters, the Kentucky Derby looked like a cavalry charge as the big field swept down the stretch and past the stands for the first time. Horses were bumped and blocked, but Velasquez steered his mount clear, taking him from 15th after six furlongs to first by the top of the stretch. He held on to win by three-quarters of a length.

Up in Baltimore two weeks later, Pleasant Colony won the Preakness. But there would be no Triple Crown for Campo and Company. An outsider named Summing saw to that in the Belmont Stakes. Pleasant Colony won once more that season in the prestigious Woodward Stakes. The horse retired to a successful stud career at Buckland Farm in Kentucky.

Gato Del Sol ✦ May 1, 1982

Cajun jockey Eddie Delahoussaye "works" Gato del Sol on a morning several days before to the 108th Derby. (Inset) Co-owners Arthur Hancock III and Leone Peters with the trophy.

In 1981 Arthur Hancock, son of the late Bull Hancock, wrote and recorded a song called "A Horse of Another Color," no doubt inspired by his gray colt. Gato Del Sol means "cat in the sun." His trainer, ex-Hollywood actor Eddie Gregson, had noticed a cat stretching in a sunny area near the stable and had decided on the Spanish translation as Gato's sire, the grass champion Cougar II, was from Chile. Gato Del Sol joined three gray Derby winners before him—Determine, Decidedly and Spectacular Bid.

The gray colt was a 21 to 1 long shot, the favorite being Air Forbes Won. In the early going he trailed the field of 19 by 16 lengths and did not appear to be a threat to any horse. But in the backstretch he began to move up. Since Judge Himes in 1903, no horse had made such a move in the Derby. He came through the traffic in the turn for home and picked off his competition as he charged down the stretch. Cupecoy's Joy, the filly who led all the way, was joined by El Baba and Air Forbes Won, but all three spit out the bit at the eighth pole and the "cat in the sun" crossed the finish line two-and-a-half lengths in front. The time for the race was a respectable 2:00⅖, and a win ticket paid $44.40, the second biggest payout since Proud Clarion in 1967.

Arthur Hancock III's father had wanted a Derby win more than anything and had bred and trained horses for all his life but never won. He came the closest in 1969 when Dike came within a half-length of Majestic Prince. At Bull Hancock's death, the executors chose his other son, Seth, to run Claiborne. Arthur established his own Stone Farm, just down the road, and with the help of Leone Peters bred, among many others, Gato Del Sol. In his acceptance speech, Arthur said, "I dedicate this Derby to Daddy."

Sunny's Halo ✦ May 7, 1983

Sunny's Halo and Eddie Delahoussaye, with shirttails flying, gallop under the wire in the 109th Kentucky Derby. A cameraman loses control in the excitement.

*I*t was not the kind of day that Stephen Foster described. Moments before the big race, as the crowd sang Foster's "My Old Kentucky Home," umbrellas went up to fend off the rain. While thousands in the infield used plastic garbage bags to keep dry, millionaires and celebrities observed the race from the climate-controlled Skye Terrace. Former presidents Gerald Ford and Jimmy Carter, Vice-President George Bush, ex-Secretary of State Henry Kissinger and Kentucky's Governor John Y. Brown with First Lady Phyllis George Brown were there to cheer the winner across the finish line. Despite the bugs in a newly installed computer wagering system and one betting machine briefly out of commission, a crowd of 134,444 wagered a record $5,546,977 to the delight of Churchill Downs' president Lynn Stone.

Sunny's Halo out of Mostly Sunny, entered the Kentucky Derby after only two starts at three, both of which he'd won—the last on April 16 in the one-and-one-eighth mile Arkansas Derby with Delahoussaye in the irons for the first time.

Twenty colts started this Derby Day. Marfa, the favorite, coupled with Balboa Native and Total Departure as the D. Wayne Lucas entry, needed discipline according to Lucas and it showed. Marfa was not a threat to Sunny's Halo and Delahoussaye who won by two lengths. After winning his second consecutive Derby, the first to do so since Ron Turcotte on Secretariat, Delahoussaye said, "God, it's a great feeling!"

Swale ✦ May 5, 1984

Oil portrait of Lafitte Pincay hand-riding Swale to win the 110th Kentucky Derby.

*I*t was late morning at Claiborne Farm in the spring of 1981, time for the foals to come in. The young son of Seattle Slew and Tuerta was nowhere to be found. Fearing the worst, Claiborne personnel searched this nation's top breeding facility only to discover the colt snoring peacefully behind a slight rise in his paddock. So it was that the record books nearly had "Foghorn" as the 1984 Kentucky Derby winner instead of that graceful name which evokes pastoral images so similar to the slews of Washington state—"Swale".

Claiborne had its origin long before the Kentucky Derby existed as Captain Richard Hancock's Virginia estate, Ellerslie, founded in the Civil War era and shifted to Kentucky by his son Arthur in 1915, the same year the filly, Regret, won the Derby and brought the race to national prominence. Born in the inaugural year of the Derby, Arthur Hancock instituted Claiborne's quest for Derby gold. The challenge was taken up by his son, "Bull" who crossed Forli with Continue but got only a disappointing one-eyed filly—Tuerta. But Tuerta's sleepy son would finally bring home the prize so avidly sought through three generations under the guidance of Bull's scholarly, introspective son, Seth.

Swale's own victories prior to the Derby had been overshadowed by the wins of his stablemate, James P. Mills' Devil's Bag, the two-year-old champ Eddie Maple chose to ride in the Derby. But Devil's Bag had to be scratched and it was Lafitte Pincay who piloted Swale through a perfect trip, clear of all the bumping of the 19 horses behind him. Swale was accelerating when he passed the roaring stands for the last time.

Swale didn't place in the Preakness but triumphed in the one-and-a-half mile Belmont Stakes. A week later, exercise rider, Ron McKenzie, was just putting his tack away after giving Swale a light workout when the colt suddenly reared and keeled over on his side. In minutes the best three-year-old in the country was dead. Although initial signs pointed to heart attack or stroke, veterinarians were never able to diagnose the cause of death. Trainer Woody Stephens said the colt never had any medications, was never sick a day and never missed a workout in his short life. "He broke my heart," said McKenzie.

Spend a Buck ✦ May 4, 1985

Close-up of Spend a Buck being led back to the winner's circle. Inset of his trainer, the unassuming Cam Gambolati.

*D*ennis Diaz hardly had to "spend a buck" to acquire this spectacular winner of the 1985 Derby. Purchased for $12,500 as a yearling, he came under the charge of trainer Cam Gambolati who had just taken over as full trainer for Florida-based Norman St. Leon. Foaled in Kentucky, but not in the Blue Grass region, Spend a Buck's two-year-old victories came at what were not the most glamorous tracks. However, they led to the Breeder's Cup Juvenile where he ran third, even though he suffered from a bone chip. This problem was corrected, and he recovered in Davie, Florida, not the more fashionable Ocala. Like many before him, this Kentucky Derby winner's road to the Roses was not paved with gold, proving that horses will be horses despite all the careful planning, breeding, syndications and politics. The good ones sometimes pop up wherever they please.

Two months after his knee operation, Spend a Buck was back on the track ready for his three-year old season. His first win was a 10-length victory. His second, just two weeks prior to the Derby, he won by nine-and-a-half lengths, just missing Secretariat's record for a mile-and-an-eighth by a second.

Stephen's Odyssey started late and was boxed in, leaving Angel Cordero to take Spend a Buck to the lead before passing under the wire the first time. Spend a Buck was playing, hopping shadows, while blasting away from the field. In the backstretch he widened his lead to six lengths. Watching from the stands, Diaz and Gambolati could only gasp in astonishment. Even Cordero thought there must be another horse hiding close behind him. Spend a Buck's first three-quarter mile was the fastest in Derby history, including Secretariat's. His winning time was just one-fifth off Northern Dancer's and four-fifths off Secretariat's, but neither of those horses led wire to wire.

Instead of taking the traditional road to the Triple Crown via the Preakness and Belmont Stakes, Diaz and Gambolati opted for the more lucrative $2.6 million Jersey Derby, the Monmouth, Cherry Hill and Garden State Stakes (with its $2 million bonus), all of which Spend a Buck won and finished his career with a grand cash total of $4,220,689—337 times Diaz's original investment of $12,500!

Ferdinand ✦ *May 3, 1986*

Ears forward and still looking fresh, Ferdinand takes the 112th Derby. Inset: 73-year-old trainer Charlie Whittingham and 54-year-old jockey Bill Shoemaker.

The scenario of the 112th Kentucky Derby winner could not have been more different from the 111th. Where Spend a Buck's pedigree was acceptable, Ferdinand's was impeccable, with Nijunsky II, Northern Dancer and Nearctic on his sire's side and several generations back, Dark Star, the only horse to beat Native Dancer, on his mother's side. Thirty years prior to this Derby, Ferdinand's owner, multi-millionaire Howard Keck of California, began his breeding business with the help of Bull Hancock of Claiborne. Having had so many stakes winners on the West Coast, the Derby was never a quest for Keck or trainer Charlie Whittingham, who chose to start horses later in their two-year-old seasons. Having run only two horses in the Derby that didn't place, 73-year-old Whittingham determined not to enter again unless he had a horse who could win. His 17 to 1 shot with the lackluster name would live up to his promise.

Bill Shoemaker filled the irons this first Saturday in May and at 54 years of age, there was never kinder, wiser jockey. He knew the track well, having ridden in 24 Derbies and won three. Whittingham, when asked why he had selected such an old jockey, responded, "Well, he's not so old. I'm 73!"

Just out of the gate several horses came over on Ferdinand, nearly throwing him down, but Shoemaker held him together. Coming off the turn for home, experience would pay off again as Shoemaker saw a hole develop on the inside and went for it instantly. The 54-year-old threw caution to the wind and rode with the bravery of a kid. With no Derby win in 21 years, "the Shoe" wasn't about to let Ferdinand think about tiring. Shoe sat down and drove his horse home two-and-a-half lengths in front. The old-time racetracker admitted to a "tear or two" as they galloped back to the winner's circle.

The handsome chestnut colt with the profile of an Arabian would run second in the Preakness and third in the Belmont, first in the Breeder's Cup Classic and continue at five to bring home large purses, proving out the wisdom of Whittingham's style to the end.

Alysheba ✦ May 2, 1987

Close-up of one of the best-looking horses to win the Derby.

*P*reston Madden bred this handsome son of Alydar at Hamburg Place which had produced five Derby winners starting with Old Rosebud, then Sir Barton, Paul Jones, Zev and Flying Ebony. Forty years after assuming management of Hamburg, Madden had his first Derby winner in Dorothy Scarbauer's Alysheba and offered this comment: "The horse business in not as difficult as it seems. If you are willing to devote all your time, effort and money to it and you live long enough—you might get lucky."

Yet, Hall-of-Fame trainer Jack van Berg was so confident of his "superhorse" he predicted in a speech in January that if nothing went wrong Alysheba would win in May. But many things did go wrong. Six weeks after his speech, van Berg had to opt for standing surgery on Alysheba's blocked windpipe or give up all plans for the Derby. Worth $5 million at that point, one slip of Dr. Merrell's scalpel on the fractious colt would have changed a lot of plans. Nine days from the Derby, Jack van Berg's supercolt had run in only two races since his public prediction, had only one lifetime win seven months prior and had recently survived surgery. "Aly" did not exactly impress three-time Jockey of the Year Greg McCarron; however, van Berg's enthusiasm swayed him.

Alysheba's road to the wire was as full of pitfalls as his road to Kentucky. Recently recovered from his first serious injury, McCarron had to stare down the face of death three times. In the first turn, horses pushed Herb McCauley on War over the rail. "My horse was actually leaning over the top of the rail with half his body," McCauley later said. Boxed in just behind them was McCarron on Alysheba, holding his breath—if War went down so would they.

McCarron and Aly then looped the field on the outside. On the turn for home they took a bead on the leader, Bet Twice. Bet Twice came over on Alysheba twice, nearly throwing him to the ground, yet the great Aly prevailed. Alysheba earned $7 million before a long, successful stud career at Lanes End Farm in Kentucky.

Winning Colors ✦ May 7, 1988

Only the third mare to win the Derby, Winning Colors refuses to give up her lead to Forty-Niner. Inset: Trainer D. Wayne Lucas

*I*t was no accident that trainer D. Wayne Lucas would pick a jockey with a good attitude to ride his great roan filly in the Kentucky Derby; he hired only clear-headed people for his meticulous training barn and that positive atmosphere attracted former San Diego Chargers owner Eugene V. Klein. Only five years into their collaboration, with $40 million in horse purchases and $300,000 in training bills per month, Klein and Lucas won the Kentucky Derby with this mottled gray filly with a colt's body, only the third female winner after Regret in 1915 and Genuine Risk in 1980. Klein choked up when interviewed after her win.

But Regret and Genuine Risk were not the favorites going into their races. Having raced just six times prior to the Derby, Winning Colors had won five, lost one by a neck only and had made hash of her male rivals in her last race, the Santa Anita Derby, where she flew in front of the boys the entire way and won by seven lengths.

Lucas had to hide his emotions when he first saw her at the Keeneland sales so as not to tip his hand before the bidding. Even so, he had to commit $575,000 of Klein's budget to get her. From the first, his son, Jeff, became attached to the high-spirited filly and Lucas let Jeff take over her training but kept a watchful eye from afar.

In the paddock the talk among trainers centered on how best to deal with this runaway filly. True to form, Winning Colors broke on top and dominated the race. Gary Stevens was cruising alone to the wire on his mare when he was surprised by Pat Day on Forty-Niner who had started their quarter-mile dash from the final turn and linked up with the filly in the last furlong. Both tired horses battled toward the finish, but the filly never lost her lead and won by a neck.

Winning Colors went on to the Preakness, where she ran third, but failed to place in the Belmont Stakes. She did triple her purchase price in earnings, however, before her retirement. Gainesway Farm bought her twice as a broodmare—for $4 million five years later.

229

Sunday Silence ✦ *May 6, 1989*

Having won the Derby, Sunday Silence is shown here winning the Preakness.
He would, however, be denied the Belmont and the Triple Crown.

*H*all-of-Fame trainer Charlie Whittingham (Ferdinand's Trainer for the 1986 Derby) learned not to rush a horse's education from his apprenticeship with the great Horatio Luro. Where he picked up his business acumen is a mystery, but the 76-year-old faired well on Sunday Silence. He originally purchased a half-interest in the two-year-old from Arthur Hancock III for $25,000, then sold half of the half to Dr. Ernest Gaillard for $25,000, cutting his cost on the horse to zero. A year after he won the Derby, quarter-interest in Sunday Silence was sold to a Japanese breeder for $2.5 million. Although the price for the whole horse was undisclosed, it's safe to say the other three-quarter interest was of like value: therefore, the return on Whittingham's quarter, which cost him nothing, was $2.5 million; the good doctor made back 1,000 percent on his investment; and Hancock, who paid only $17,000 for Sunday Silence, was also quite pleased (Sunday Silence's lifetime earnings of $5 million not included).

This spectacular son of Halo won 9 of 14 career races, including the Preakness, and was never worse than second. Just edged out in the Belmont, he nearly became the 11th Triple Crown winner since Affirmed in 1978.

Arthur Hancock III, who raised the colt, was a bit of a renegade. Splitting away from his family's illustrious Claiborne Farm, the natural songwriter and musician established his own Stone Farm. Despite his success (he bred 1982 Derby winner onto Del Sol) the superstitious Hancock combed the grass for, and found, a four-leafed clover the morning of the Derby.

The black colt's triumph in this muddy Derby was no act of chance. He earned it all the way. Off to a typically rough start, Sunday Silence sat fourth for most of the race and wore down the favorite, Ogden Phipps Easy Goer, who hung on gamely for second place. In the stretch, the torrent of noise from both stands and infield spooked him and he tangoed first left, then right, then left with Valenzuela correcting him all the way.

Although Whittingham had refrained from an actual prediction of victory, he did admit after the race that he thought his horse was a cinch to win. In this case it certainly paid to know his horse.

231

Unbrilled and Craig Perret, coming on strong. Inset: 92-year-old Frances Genter cheers on first Derby winner.

At the center of the post-Derby celebration sat an elderly lady in a wheelchair, a single bud from Unbridled's rose blanket in her lap. Ninety-two-year-old Frances Genter, who with her husband, Harold, owned and bred some of the best stakes winners in this country had finally won the Kentucky Derby. Unbridled's trainer, Carl Nafzger, called the race for his petite, white-haired client whose sight and hearing were dimmed by age. Her face glowed with wonder as she heard of Unbridled's charge to the wire. Then came Nafzger's now famous final exhuberation: "You've won the Kentucky Derby! Oh, Mrs. Genter, I love you!"

Starting with their first stakes winner, Swiv, in 1941, the Genters produced and raced numerous champions, notable among them My Dear Girl, named for Mr. Genter's gentle endearment for his wife, In Reality and Superbity; however, injuries and illnesses kept Genter horses out of the Derby until 1990.

Unbridled's success focused attention on the growing prominence of Florida racing. Genter horses were bred and trained in Ocala and started at South Florida tracks. After an on-again off-again two-year-old season, Unbridled won the Florida Derby but ran only third in the Blue Grass Stakes. Jockey Craig Perret later referred to their ride in the Derby as the "golden trip." Despite heavy going, Unbridled ran a perfect race, and won by three-and-a-half lengths. Viewing the tape later, with the emotional call of the race by Nafzger to Mrs. Genter, losing jockeys and trainers conceded that Mrs. Genter was meant to have her Derby despite their disappointment.

Unbridled nearly won the Preakness, and in November prevailed in the $3 million Breeder's Cup Classic. Mrs. Genter was honored as Woman of the Year on her birthday and passed on leaving Unbridled to carry on the Genter legend.

Strike the Gold ✦ May 4, 1991

Strike the Gold works out at Churchill Downs prior to the Derby. Inset: Trainer Nick Zito.

Nicholas Philip Zito sat at the country bus station in Middleburg, Virginia, with $20 in his pocket and a ticket to New York. The kid from Queens had returned to Middleburg with Trainer Woods Garth after the Keeneland meet, but wasn't ready for the genteel life. Once back in New York, he worked with Leroy Jolley before striking out on his own with one horse, Big Red Devil, his meal ticket for two years. Times were tough. Greentree trainer John Gaver happened to see Zito walking down a backstretch road in search of a stall and took him in. It was all uphill from there. New York attitude and moxy, plus a great eye for a good horse, paved Zito's way up the ladder that would end at the winner's platform—not only this Derby but again in 1994 with Go for Gin.

Fellow New Yorkers Giles Brophy, Joseph Cornacchia and William Condren were successful businessmen with virtually no experience with horses. Zito's stakes winner, Warfie, attracted the interest of Brophy and he gave him $500,000 to go buy horses. From that collaboration came Thirty-Six-Red, a million-dollar winner in 1990 and Condren and Cornachia joined the team.

Strike the Gold, a handsome son of the great Alydar sadly put to sleep in 1990, experienced his own mis fortune at birth. The foal had to be put on oxygen and fed through a tube for three days before he could fend for himself. Benefitting from recent hock treatment, Strike the Gold and jockey Chris Antley defeated Fly So Free by three lengths in the Blue Grass Stakes and Derby Day would see them pitted against each other again. Fly So Free tired and the horse to beat was Best Pal with Gary Stevens who thought he had it won at the eighth pole until he saw Strike the Gold flying down the middle of the track. Gold kept drifting but he cruised under the wire one-and-three-quarter lengths ahead of Best Pal.

Back at Calumet, John Ginn, Gold's groom in the early days, held Gold's first pair of shoes and saw the foal once again outrunning his playmates across the blue-green waves of endless Kentucky meadow.

Lil E.T. ✦ *May 2, 1992*

Pat Day celebrates as he wins on the 17 to 1 shot, Lil E.T.

The 118th Kentucky Derby is the story of the "lil" guy. Named for his breeder's initials (Lawrence I. Littman) and his nickname as a foal, Lil E.T. was born on a 36-acre breeding farm in New Jersey, small enough for a manager to give foals nicknames. He was sold for a small price, $2,000, as a yearling considered not good enough for the Ocala Breeder's Sales and bought by Cal Rantee, a self-made man from a small town in Arkansas, after he saw the colt win by 11 lengths. Lynn Whiting was a hard-knocking trainer who ran his horses in the Midwest. Their Kentucky Derby victory sent a message to the bulk of horsemen who toil far from the limelight that the great ones can come to anyone.

Lil E.T. was a "huge, gangly colt with high knee action and high-headedness and not a good mover," according to farm manager Mary Deppa, "with a habit of losing his mother and screaming for her." Deppa would joke, "There's E.T. phoning home again," and the name stuck. As a yearling, he underwent major surgery for a twisted intestine and in an accident nearly lost one ear. Nevertheless, the ugly duckling grew into a swan that put to shame all the pricey and famous favorites on Derby Day.

Lil E.T. went to post with odds of 17 to 1. Among the more colorful entrants were rap-star Hammer's Dance Floor; Technology, winner of the Florida Derby; Devil His Due, winner of the Gotham; Arkansas Derby winner Pine Bluff; Blue Grass Stakes winner Pistols and Roses; and what was dubbed the "most glamorous animal on earth," Arazi, winner of the Breeder's Cup Juvenile, who brought his throng of adoring fans with him wherever he ran. There was no clear favorite, however. Somehow, Lil E.T.'s victory in the $500,000 Jim Beam Stakes was overlooked. Pat Day was not about to forget it. With his choice of rides and nine previous attempts to win the Roses, Day still stuck with E.T.

True to the tone of this tale, all the big guys got stuck in the muck, the footing so deep one jockey likened it to the Sahara Desert. The hard-working little guys toughed it out among themselves. Not one of the three horses that finished immediately behind E.T. went off with odds better than 20 to 1.

Sea Hero ✦ May 1, 1993

Sea Hero leads the pack to win for Paul Mellon and trainer MacKenzie Miller.

Sea Hero won the Kentucky Derby on one of his better days, benefitting from the wise choices of his trainer, Mack Miller, and his rider, Jerry Bailey, who waited for a hole between horses and went for it. But the real heroes were Paul Mellon, an unassuming 85-year-old megamillionaire and kind gentleman, and his sportsmanlike trainer, 71-year-old Mackenzie Miller. The phrase rippling through the crowd seconds after the horse with the Seattle Slew bridle flew under the wire was, "It couldn't have happened to a nicer guy." They meant Paul Mellon and they meant Mackenzie Miller.

Sea Hero was magnificent, but his biggest accomplishment was garnering this cherished trophy for two men who had deserved it all their lives. Paul Mellon spent a life giving and racing: the Mellon National Gallery of Art in Washington, D.C., the Skeaping bronze of Secretariat in Belmont's paddock, the Middleburg Training Center are but some of his $1 billion in charitable donations. His own Brickhouse Museum at Rokeby Farm in Upperville, Virginia, is a storehouse of international art treasures. Rokeby produced the racing greats Quadrangle, Arts and Letters, Mill Reef and Horses of the Year Fort Marcy and Key to the Mint. Mellon could be seen on a rainy day driving his tractor at Rokeby or at a local point-to-point race, genuinely involved with his horses. He well earned the title of nicest rich guy on earth.

This Derby win was bittersweet for Mellon. Sensing the reality of his numbered days, he had recently dispersed all his horses. The incredibly manicured stone barns echoed with emptiness. What a nice time for Mellon to be rewarded for his illustrious racing career.

MacKenzie Miller, a soft-spoken Kentuckian boy, enjoyed a 40-year career in racing. He was a gentleman to a fault who said after the race, "I'm not important. I'm so pleased for my boss." As so often happens in the Derby, the right people with the right horse win at the right time.

Go for Gin ◆ May 7, 1994

Greg McCarron is jubilant as Go for Gin is led to the winner's circle.

"Some things you work hard for and they never happen and some things are just meant to be," said Nick Zito as he accepted congratulations for this Derby with the memory of Strike the Gold's 1991 win fresh in everyone's mind. Having won two out of three Derbies, his win rate was bested only by the joint owners of both winners, Bill Condren and Joe Cornacchia who got into the "game" just a few years before their first Derby triumph.

Typical of so many Derby races, the expected never happened and in this one the unexpected was all that happened. Holy Bull was considered a cinch to win. Second place favorites were Brocco, Tabasco Cat and Blumin' Affair. Charlie Whittingham's Strodes Creek was a big question mark. Not only had he never won a race, he never raced at two, period. But everyone suspected, as Zito so poetically put in, "Charlie's not here for the Kentucky air."

At the bell, the horses spilled out of the gate like ants out of a matchbox, colliding and scattering; all except Brocco, the only serious challenge to Holy Bull, who just stood there mesmerized by the crowd, and Holy Bull who broke late and never really recovered. Go for Gin broke straight and was mercifully free of the melee behind him. He never looked back.

Greg McCarron, Alysheba's winning jockey in 1987, had earned a reputation as the best "pick-up" rider in the business and his knack for communicating with a horse quickly paid off here. He exercised Go for Gin for the first time just days before the Derby. When the horse broke on top and didn't want to relax, Greg had the good sense to let him go for it.

After the race, Zito gave credit to Go for Gin's groom and exercise rider, who knew his horse best. "You're only as good as your help," said the man who started as a hot-walker and continued to bathe and cool out his own horses throughout his career. "You've got to work hard and keep working . . . never lose your love for this business and good things will happen for you." And perhaps the most telling pre-Derby quote from this boy from Queens with the best win record in the country, "My dad told us to always remember, the underdog is a dangerous animal."

Index

255